LEAVING PHARAOH'S HOUSE

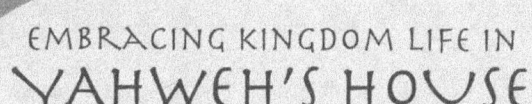

EMBRACING KINGDOM LIFE IN YAHWEH'S HOUSE

SHANE CALLICUTT

Copyright © 2019 by Shane Callicutt

All rights reserved. No part of this publication may be reproduced, distributed, or transmitted in any form or by any means, including photocopying, recording, or other electronic or mechanical methods, without the prior written permission of the publisher, except in the case of brief quotations embodied in critical reviews and certain other noncommercial uses permitted by copyright law. For permission requests, contact the author via the website listed below.

www.shaneshack.com

Unless otherwise noted, all Scripture quotations are from the ESV® Bible (The Holy Bible, English Standard Version®), copyright © 2001 by Crossway, a publishing ministry of Good News Publishers. Used by permission. All rights reserved.

Scripture taken from the New King James Version® (NKJV). Copyright © 1982 by Thomas Nelson. Used by permission. All rights reserved.

Any **bold** or *italicized* words within Scripture quotations have been added by the author for emphasis.

Thanks, once again, to Cathy for reviewing this in your spare time. Your insights and encouragement are invaluable.

Radene, you have endured yet another season of writing. You journey with me, you uphold me, you love me, and if I didn't have you with me, I'm sure that I would be a much sadder, boring, less pleasant, more serious version of myself.

Based on feedback about the original book released on October 5, 2019, this is a revised edition, containing the added elements of breaks and headings within the chapters that will make your reading experience a little easier.

TABLE OF CONTENTS

INTRODUCTION 1

Chapter 1
PHARAOH'S HOUSE 5

Chapter 2
THE ENEMY OF UNITY 33

Chapter 3
THE DEVIL'S IN THE DETAILS 69

Chapter 4
JESUS TRUMPS 103

Chapter 5
SEEDS OF RECONCILIATION 135

Chapter 6
LOVING THROUGH 169

Chapter 7
YAHWEH'S HOUSE 201

CONCLUSION 233

INTRODUCTION

My heart has been heavy with the content of this book for a while now. I'm a worship pastor, so I don't get many consecutive opportunities to preach. That's one reason I write books because it gives me an outlet for expressing what the Lord is doing in my heart. But this book is different for me. As much as *Recreated* and *Renewed* were birthed out of my own personal experiences, this one comes from a different place.

The Lord has taken me on a very personal journey as I've put words on paper for this book. I can't explain it to you. Without fail, it's as if every thought that I've written down has gone through testing. I feel like Jesus has been double checking my work the whole time.

Oh, that's what you believe… let's test that.

Because of that, this book has been a labor of passion, unlike the others. You can be assured of this: if it made it into this book, it has been tested by fire.

The heart of this book is all about embracing what it means to be a member of Yahweh's house. It's about what we must lose to live as sons and daughters of the Living God. Too many Christians are too bound to this world to be good ambassadors of Jesus. That's not me being critical or judgy against others. That's an indictment on my own faith journey. And so it is for most of us.

As we march forward, inching ever closer to the return of Christ, the days are going to get darker. More now than ever, the Body of Christ desperately needs to display the power of God. We can spin our wheels asking God to show his might, but we deny him the opportunities to do it when we keep one foot in Pharaoh's house and one foot in Yahweh's house.

Moses lived that way up until he was forty years old, and what I hope to demonstrate to you is how the comforts of Pharaoh's house was an anchor that prevented Moses from moving forward to fulfill his destiny as a deliverer for God's people. I also hope to show you that we aren't any different.

I'm going to be straight with you. You're going to read some hard things in the pages ahead. This may challenge you in ways that might make you uncomfortable. You may even be tempted to write me off on a few of these issues as naïve or a little too *out there*. That's alright. As I wrote this, it slowly dawned on me that I'm actually barking up a lot of trees that belong to faithful churchgoers. Then it occurred to me that this could possibly cause some of those faithful churchgoers to squirm a bit. And after that, it occurred to me... I'm ok with that. I'm not writing this to be anything except honest about where God has me, what he's showing me, and how it applies to what I'm observing within the Body of Christ.

What will it take for you to pack up your things in Pharaoh's house and cast your everything into the kingdom of God? Yahweh's house is our home. Let's take an honest look into why we keep dwelling in Pharaoh's house where we don't belong.

INTRODUCTION

PHARAOH'S HOUSE

Now the daughter of Pharaoh came down to bathe at the river, while her young women walked beside the river. She saw the basket among the reeds and sent her servant woman, and she took it. When she opened it, she saw the child, and behold, the baby was crying. She took pity on him and said, "This is one of the Hebrews' children." Then his sister said to Pharaoh's daughter, "Shall I go and call you a nurse from the Hebrew women to nurse the child for you?" And Pharaoh's daughter said to her, "Go." So the girl went and called the child's mother. And Pharaoh's daughter said to her, "Take this child away and nurse him for me, and I will give you your wages." So the woman took the child and nursed him. When the child grew older, she brought him to Pharaoh's daughter, and he became her son. She named him Moses, "Because," she said, "I drew him out of the water."

One day, when Moses had grown up, he went out to his people and looked on their burdens, and he saw an Egyptian beating a Hebrew, one of his people. He looked this way and that, and seeing no one, he struck down the Egyptian and hid him in the sand. When he went out the next day, behold, two Hebrews were struggling together. And he said to the man in the wrong, "Why do you strike your companion?" He answered, "Who made you a prince and a judge over us? Do you mean to kill me as you killed the Egyptian?" Then Moses was afraid, and thought, "Surely the thing is known." When Pharaoh heard of it, he sought to kill Moses. But Moses fled from Pharaoh and stayed in the land of Midian. And he sat down by a well. (Exodus 2:5-15)

It's a familiar story to billions. Whether you learned this in Sunday School on a flannel board, or by watching the movies *The Prince of Egypt* or *The Ten Commandments*, or by parents who read the Scripture to you growing up, the story of Moses is a treasured account, even to multiple religions. This will be an attempt to tell you how this small passage from Exodus has been methodically tearing down and rebuilding how I understand my life.

It's a strange passage for someone to lay claim to as *life-changing*. In the span of eleven verses what you get is an insanely brief overview of nearly forty years of the life of Moses; not much space for details. At this moment I'm almost forty-two years old. If you were to read a biography of my life, written in the same way as the first forty years of Moses' life you'd get something like this.

> Now, Shane was born to Kent and Cheryl, who lived in the state of Mississippi. He was born with respiratory problems, of which the doctors gave little hope for him surviving. By the Lord's intervention, Shane lived. A short time later Kent and Cheryl divorced. Cheryl's father and mother, Herman and Lois, adopted Shane and his sisters. Cheryl married again to a man named Dennis, and she continued to be an active part of

her children's lives. And as he grew, Shane was always reminded of the miracle the Lord worked to save his life, being told constantly, "The Lord has a plan for your life."

One day when Shane had grown up, moved to Colorado, gotten married to Radene, had two daughters, Phoebe and Ayva, and then moved to Missouri to serve the Lord, he began writing books about his love for Jesus.

And that would be about it to cover my first forty years in the same kind of detail as the Bible does for Moses. So much is left unsaid. So much happened between *the Lord has a plan for your life* and *one day when Shane had grown up*. It's completely lacking for anything that would help you understand my adult years, and it's also an unfair account of my infant and toddler years because it leaves out so much nuance that would help you understand everything that happened between my parents' divorce and my adoption. In some respects, that's what we have with Moses: a very brief telling of his formative years and nothing about his young adulthood. That leaves us with more questions than answers. However, it's in between the lines of these eleven verses where the Holy Spirit has been unearthing truths that are reshaping me as a young, middle-aged adult.

In the retellings of the story of Moses which we've seen on the silver screen, some of them dive deep into speculation about his upbringing in the Egyptian royal court. After all, he was adopted by Pharaoh's daughter, making him a grandson to Pharaoh. Being a grandson to Pharaoh certainly comes with its privileges. While Hollywood has taken its liberties with this phase of Moses' life, it's helpful to remember that it is speculation; informed speculation, but speculation nonetheless (how well informed depends on the writers and directors' efforts).

In these opening pages what I'd like to do with you is engage in a bit of our own speculation. Nothing wild, nothing without basis, but rather some truth-based examination of what likely happened to Moses during those unwritten years of his life. I'll do my best to keep this interesting so stick with me through this because it will set the course for the remainder of this volume.

Just in case you've never read the story of Moses, let me give you a quick, condensed history. In Genesis chapter twelve, God begins a covenant with an old man named Abram, later renamed Abraham, to give him descendants and land for them to possess as their own.

God fulfilled his promise to Abraham by giving him a son, named Isaac (Genesis 21). Isaac had twin (fraternal) sons, Esau and Jacob (Genesis 26). Jacob deceived his father to steal Esau's firstborn blessing, so Jacob received the firstborn blessing from his father, though he was second-born (Genesis 27). Jacob, who was later renamed Israel (Genesis 32), fathers twelve sons (Genesis 35). Israel's son, Joseph, is disliked among his brothers, so they sold him to merchants as a slave (Genesis 37).

Joseph was sold as a slave in Egypt, but God was with him and blessed him (Genesis 39). Even though his journey in Egypt wasn't always smooth, eventually he gained favor with Pharaoh and was made governor of all Egypt, second only to Pharaoh himself (Genesis 41). Joseph's wise handling of the affairs of Egypt prepared them for a drought, ensuring that Egypt would not be without food throughout the famine (Genesis 41).

The famine was so severe and widespread that it drove Joseph's brothers to travel to Egypt for food, where through a series of tests, they were reunited with Joseph (Genesis 42-45). Because of the authority Joseph possessed in Egypt, he granted the land of Goshen to his family and urged them to move to Egypt until the famine was over (Genesis 45-47). And Israel and his sons remained in Egypt.

At the beginning of Exodus, we learn that Israel remained in Egypt for over four hundred years. But toward the end of that time, a new Pharaoh rose to power who feared the nation of Israel and had no respect for Joseph's family. The Israelites were very numerous, so Pharaoh enslaved them and commanded that all their newborn boys be killed (Exodus 1). To protect their son from Pharaoh's decree, Amram and Jochebed (pronounced yo-keh'-bed), put Moses in a basket coated with tar and pitch and set him afloat in the Nile river. That is where we pick up the story in detail at Exodus 2:5.

NO ORDINARY BATH

Pharaoh's daughter is bathing in the Nile. Don't take this for granted. She wouldn't simply get in the Nile to take her daily bath as we might think. The Nile river was sacred to the Egyptians.[1] Its waters were considered divine, so the bathing we read about here probably wasn't ordinary. In all likelihood, it was a part of some religious observance.[2] So get this in your head: the princess was in a mindset of worship as she entered the divine waters of the Nile. She might've been praying or chanting as she entered the waters. If so, then this wasn't a leisurely bath but rather an act of worship to Hapi, one of Egypt's gods that were associated with the Nile River.

As she worshiped while entering the sacred waters, she spotted the basket. After having one of her maidservants retrieve it, she opened it and discovered baby Moses within. Think about it. Hapi was believed to bring life to the Nile valley when he flooded the region with fertile soil from the river's sediments. She found a baby afloat in the sacred waters of the Nile while worshiping Hapi. She may have understood this as a divine event. She recognized the baby as Hebrew, yet she didn't call for the guards to take him and throw him in the Nile as Pharaoh had ordered be done to all Hebrew boys. His cries stirred her compassion. Perhaps something in her knew this boy was special; after all, he came to her in what was for her a sacred moment.

This leads me to an essential subpoint of the story. Our God, Yahweh, frequently uses the plans and schemes of the other gods to move his own plan forward. Perhaps, in this case, Yahweh used the reverence that Pharaoh's daughter had for Hapi to preserve Moses' life. And later in the Exodus story, Yahweh uses the ten plagues to shame the Egyptian gods, demonstrating his superior power over them.[3] In fact, the Word says as much.

while the Egyptians were burying all their firstborn, whom the Lord had struck down among them. *On their gods also the Lord executed judgments.* (Numbers 33:4)

To understand the worldview of the Scripture, you must embrace a supernatural understanding of the world around us. If the only thing you see in the Scripture is the human struggle to be reconciled with its Creator, then you're missing a large piece of the mosaic. When we gave in to the serpent's temptation in Eden, we were drawn into a larger cosmic struggle. So now we are either pawns of the gods who oppose Yahweh, or we are participants actively fighting against those gods. If your worldview is anything less than that, then you'll find the Word of God to be irrational at times and difficult to reconcile with what you've chosen to believe.

The problem with many professing Christians is they embrace a sub-spiritual understanding of Scripture, or perhaps better put they are selectively supernatural. They'll welcome the supernatural when it comes to things like the virgin birth, the resurrection, and miracles worked by Jesus and the Apostles, but the rest strains credulity. Biblically understanding the world means that you accept there are powers at work in an unseen world where Yahweh is patiently working out his plan to subdue all other spiritual powers who oppose him. And this struggle spills over into the seen world because part of Yahweh's plan to conquer his foes is to redeem humanity through Jesus Christ to the power and position for which he created us.

Believers in Jesus Christ have no need to fear the supernatural. Don't allow that word to conjure up images of the guy who's looking for demons under every rock and throwing oil over everything because he's *afraid* of the demonic. While those individuals do exist, they're caricatures of reality. They exaggerate the truth, they embrace a super-spirituality that's more superstitious than Christian, and Satan is happy to let them walk in that kind of fear. If you belong to Christ that kind of superstitious belief needs to be torn down along with every other stronghold that has fortified your mind. To be clear, sometimes there are demons under rocks that need to be uncovered, and there are times to anoint people with oil and pray for them. But as Spirit-filled believers, we follow his leading in those things rather than a superstitious fear of Satan. As long as we walk in the light (1 John 1:7), we need not fear the darkness.

Therefore, embracing a supernatural mindset helps us see that even the simplicity of finding Moses in the river waters was turning the tables on the gods that oppose Yahweh and his plan to redeem humanity. Moving on.

What's next is interesting: Moses' sister, Miriam, was closely keeping an eye on the basket from a distance. Clearly, she loved her little brother and wanted to do what she could to ensure his safety. As soon as Pharaoh's daughter decided that she would keep him, Miriam spoke up and offered to find a nursing woman from the Hebrews to nurse him. Now, who do you think she was going to choose? Ding! Ding! Ding! Jochebed, their mother, is the correct answer! So, Miriam summons Jochebed, and get this: Pharaoh's daughter offers to pay Moses' mother to nurse him: *"Take this child away and nurse him for me, **and I will give you your wages**."* So not only did Yahweh turn the tables on Hapi and use the princess' devotion to spare Moses, who would eventually be God's instrument to deliver his people from Egypt, but he also worked out things so that Jochebed would be paid to do something that she would've naturally done for no pay whatsoever! Double the win, double the blessing for God's people!

Now, what comes next isn't apparent in the text. This is where we have to kind of read between the lines a bit. Jochebed took her son and nursed him, then it reads, *"When the child grew older she brought him to Pharaoh's daughter…"* How much older? We really don't know, but here's what we may be able to infer. First of all, these series of events have been orchestrated by Yahweh's careful watch. It should be no surprise to us if he allowed Moses to remain with his birth parents until such an age that he was well instructed in his Hebrew heritage. In fact, we know from just a few verses later that as an adult Moses was well aware that he was a Hebrew. Secondly, this probably isn't something Pharaoh's daughter would have instilled in him. In fact, she may have worked hard to draw very little attention to his heritage since her father had ordered Moses' generation of male Hebrew children to be killed. In Pharaoh's house, Moses' Hebrew heritage was probably never spoken of at dinner or anywhere else for that matter. Finally, by many scholarly accounts the oldest Moses could've been here is three years old.[4] If true, this makes it even more miraculous that Yahweh opened the three-year-old mind of young Moses to remember his mother's instruction about his heritage.

Here's something perhaps you've never considered. Again, something not mentioned in the story, but one can only imagine that Amram and Jochebed had already given him a proper name. A nice

Hebrew name. But as I've previously mentioned, his heritage was likely deemphasized in Pharaoh's house. Therefore, Pharaoh's daughter gave him the name that history will remember: Moses. At this point, my heart goes out to Amram and Jochebed. They have now given up their son twice, but to pile hurt on top of hurt the name they gave their son was unceremoniously replaced. Was it necessary? Yes. But that likely didn't assuage their pain. The only consolation they had was their hope that Yahweh would use their son to deliver Israel.

YEARS BETWEEN THE LINES

What happens next is epic. Between verses ten and eleven is the passage of probably thirty-seven years. How do we know this? Elsewhere in the Scripture, it is said that when Moses killed the Egyptian he was forty years old (Acts 7:23). This thirty-seven year gap in the narrative is fascinating, and we can imply a few things, but as for exactly what happened, we can't be sure. What can we suggest about Moses' life in Pharaoh's court? There are really only a few things we can say with confidence, but they're powerful things that will help us understand the magnitude of what Moses did in killing the Egyptian.

First, as the adopted grandson of Pharaoh, he would be considered royalty. This means that after his third year, he never experienced poverty. He was surrounded by wealth and affluence. The finest that Egypt could offer was commonplace in the house of Pharaoh, and his family was the immediate benefactor. A grandson of Pharaoh, especially as he grew into manhood, would be refused no good thing.

Second, Moses received a solid Egyptian education. Most of the scholars I've read agree that this was similar to what we would consider a renaissance education where a healthy grasp of many subjects was mastered. For instance, Moses received instruction in geometry and arithmetic, but he would not be considered educated enough to be an engineer. Likewise with other subjects. One commentary states, "We should do wrong to regard him as either a scientific man or a philosopher. His genius was practical; and his education was of a practical kind - such as fitted him to become the leader of his people in a great emergency, to deal on equal terms with a powerful monarch, and to guide to a happy conclusion the hazardous enterprise of a great national migration."[5]

Third, being Pharaoh's grandson put him in the line of succession to the throne. The Bible is unclear to the identity of the particular Pharaoh, so we can't be sure of his family. But in any case, if the correct sequence of tragedies befell Pharaoh's house, Moses would have been his successor. In all likelihood, Moses enjoyed a certain level of protection. Perhaps he had his own Egyptian Secret Service agents that watched over his safety. I'm only speculating here, and this is probably my most imaginative yet, but it doesn't stretch things too far to consider it.

So, this is Moses' life for about thirty-seven years: from three to forty. It's a life of luxury, comfort, excess, protection, and opportunity. He never lacked, he likely could have had any woman he wanted, and he probably never faced a situation where he didn't have some kind of a life-line that could rescue him from trouble. I don't mean to imply that he was immoral or that he was reckless with his life. I only want to draw a very human picture of the man. Many people are morally ruined by the kind of wealth he had at his disposal. And what we see happen next indicates that to some degree power and wealth had corrupted him a bit.

I don't want to be completely unfair to Moses. What happens in verse eleven through fifteen is something good and something bad. Moses heads to Goshen to check in on his people. When he witnesses an Egyptian beating one of his people, a good thing stirred within him. Moses saw an injustice being done to one of his own, and he rose up to defend him. That's good. We should all rise up against injustice when we see it. But the power and wealth he had enjoyed for so long corrupted his moral compass. Moses didn't merely stop the Egyptian, he waited until he was alone and he murdered him. The Bible says, *"He looked this way and that, and **seeing no one**, he struck down the Egyptian."* This wasn't just a crime of passion. It was premeditated. He literally thought he could get away with murder. Perhaps in his own way, he thought he could be Israel's deliverer on his own terms.

But it backfires. Apparently, Moses didn't see that he *wasn't* actually alone. Someone witnessed the murder, and it spread among the Hebrews. In fact, it spread so quickly that the very next day when Moses attempted to stop two Hebrews from fighting, it was thrown up in his face: *"Who made you a prince and a judge over us? Do you mean to kill me as you killed the Egyptian?"* And as rumors do (especially good ones) it spread fast, and it spread far, and soon even Pharaoh heard about it, which spelled the end for Moses' time in Pharaoh's house. Moses ran away to the neighboring land of Midian where he would remain for another forty years before returning to Egypt under Yahweh's leadership.

A HEART FOR THE OPPRESSED

Now, to the point. That's as far as we need to go in Moses' story to get across what I'm about to lay down. I realize that I've led you into some speculation, but I believe nothing I've shared has led anyone away from the truth. Whatever the real truth may be, I believe it is some variation of what we've just discussed. Now, all I want to talk about is Moses' decision. He made a decision that altered the course of his life. The consequences of his choice changed the history of the world. And all he did was stand up for the oppressed. I'm not condoning the murder, but I am condoning his choice to intervene for his people. Intervention, good. Murder, bad. (I'm only trying to be clear and save myself a bunch of emails.)

Notice what his intervention cost him. It cost him his position. It cost him his wealth. Whatever dreams he had for the future were now gone. Any notion he had imagined in his mind of saving his people evaporated (his notions... not Yahweh's). But most painfully, it cost him his family. Pharaoh's family had become his family. Pharaoh's daughter had been his mother. To forget about the bonds of love he had for Pharaoh's house would be shortsighted. This was probably the single most painful moment of Moses' life. And to boot, he had forty years ahead of him before Yahweh would even say a word to him to give him any hope of fulfilling the destiny that Amram and Jochebed might have instilled in him.

Standing up for the oppressed will always cost. While Moses might not have had all his motives and reasons perfectly lined up with God's, there was a spark there of knowing these were his people and at that moment he was the one with the onus to defend them. And in that, the Word foreshadows our responsibility as citizens of God's kingdom.

> Then the righteous will answer him, saying, "Lord, when did we see you hungry and feed you, or thirsty and give you drink? And when did we see you a stranger and welcome you, or naked and clothe you? And when did we see you sick or in prison and visit you?" And the King will answer them, "Truly, I say to you, **as you did it to**

one of the least of these my brothers, you did it to me." (Matthew 25:37-40)

Do nothing from selfish ambition or conceit, but in humility **count others more significant than yourselves**. Let each of you look not only to his own interests, **but also to the interests of others**. (Philippians 2:3-4)

Religion that is pure and undefiled before God, the Father, is this: **to visit orphans and widows in their affliction**, and to keep oneself unstained from the world. (James 1:27)

It's actually stunning to me that this is so easily overlooked because the Word isn't vague or unclear on this matter. Kingdom people look after each other. We care for each other. We love each other. But not only that, we give special attention to the weakest among us. The oppressed receive first preference in our midst. Jesus says, *the least of these*. James lists *orphans and widows*. In either case, the Word has in mind oppressed people. The *least of these* are powerless people. They can do little to nothing to better their situation. *Widows and orphans* were socially and economically impotent in that day, and because of that, they represent some of the most oppressed; entirely dependent on someone else to intervene for their needs. We are to serve the helpless and stand up for the oppressed because that's what Jesus did for us.

And this, my friends, is what has been ruining me for a while now. I can't speak for everyone, so I'll just speak for myself and explain to you why this wrecks me personally. This reckoning has been a long time coming for me, but about a year ago I reread the first two chapters of Exodus, and it really began to pester me: how am I any different than young Moses? It's a question that I dismissed kind of quickly because, honestly, I thought it was better suited for someone else. I'm not wealthy, I'm not privileged, I've spent my life working to provide for my family, paycheck to paycheck, saving a little, only to have some emergency consume it. I'm not young Moses.

But the question endured. What I've discovered is that I'm more like young Moses than I want to admit. Wealthy? No. But have I ever *not* eventually gotten what I wanted? Seldom. And by world standards I actually *am* wealthy. Do I have a high position? No. But if position was something I desired, I possess the social skills and intelligence to perhaps attain it. Is there anything in my world that is indeed out of my grasp? And I have to answer that with a reluctant *no*. Don't mistake me for being grossly overconfident. I'm speaking strictly from odds and probability for men in my demographic. The nation I call home affords me the freedom to chase after any goal I set for myself. An early forty-something, college educated, reasonably healthy male in this nation still has much potential to accomplish whatever he decides to do. While I may not actually possess what young Moses did, my potential to reach for and even attain something like it remains.

Clearly, I have made a choice to follow Jesus, which has led me in a different direction than position, power, and affluence. And I have no regrets about it. But being a worship pastor and being given the opportunity to teach, preach, and write books has afforded me a small platform. It's not too big, but nonetheless, some people have placed faith and trust in me to lead them. Christ called me to this; it wasn't my idea. I take no credit for having whatever small amount of influence I do have. But even the good things that result from God's calling on my life can quickly become too precious.

WHAT WILL IT TAKE?

Therefore, I pose the question to myself, and to all of us: am I willing to abandon all of it in defense of the least of these? Am I willing to take a stand for the oppressed, and risk everything I hold dear as Moses did? Why do you think Moses hid the slain Egyptian's body in the ground? Because if discovered he knew his action would cost him more than he wanted to pay. And today is no different. It still requires taking up the cause of people who suffer injustice.

This is more than merely giving lip service to hating the sex slave trade, or telling the world how unprejudiced you are because you have so many friends of different colors. Anyone can make those declarations, including parrots. And I'm not trying to make anyone feel bad for stating their beliefs with sincerity. But there are people who declare things, and there are people who take action. People who take action have practiced one thing which provides the required motivation.

Empathy. Empathizing is what Moses did at the moment he rushed in to defend his Hebrew brother. He felt his pain, he felt the injustice and did something (again, to be clear I'm not condoning murder). And what I've seen not just in myself, but in many Christians is an unwillingness to do the hard work of empathizing with the struggles of the oppressed. I'm not talking about empathizing with people you already love. And neither is Jesus – although we should empathize with everyone. But we are guilty of selective empathy, which is the same thing as showing favoritism.

> If you really fulfill the royal law according to the Scripture, "You shall love your neighbor as yourself," you are doing well. But if you show partiality, you are committing sin and are convicted by the law as transgressors.
> (James 2:8-9)

> If you love those who love you, what benefit is that to you? For even sinners love those who love them. And if you do good to those who do good to you, what benefit is that to you? For even sinners do the same.
> (Luke 6:32-33)

Jesus is clear. You don't distinguish yourself as a citizen of Yahweh's kingdom if the only people you love are people who love you back. If the only people we take the time and effort to empathize with are those who already love us, how are we any different from the rest of the world?

Let me cross over from teaching into meddling. I've seen what professing Christians share on Facebook. I've read many of your Facebook posts. I've seen the Tweets you retweet. One day it's all *Jesus, Jesus, Jesus* and the next day it's *libtards, idiots, demoncrats, feminazis,* and other adjectives employed that express your hatred for the *liberal agenda* that's indoctrinating our children. Let me quote James again.

> From the same mouth come **blessing** and **cursing**. My brothers, **these things ought not to be so**. (James 3:10)

If you profess Christ and claim to be a new creation – in progress for sure, but still new – then your mouth needs to be kept in check. James says that the small flame of the tongue can set a whole forest ablaze (James 3:5), but get this: the tongue is first set afire by the powers of hell.

> And the tongue is a fire, a world of unrighteousness. The tongue is set among our members, staining the whole body, setting on fire the entire course of life, **and set on fire by hell**. (James 3:6)

If you have a loose tongue... no, let's put it in more relatable terms. If you're one of those people who claim to have no filter, beware. You are probably being used by the powers of hell to destroy other people. *The tongue is a fire, a world of unrighteousness.*

What does this have to do with empathy? I'm glad you asked. Empathic people are listeners. They are learners. They have control of what comes out of their mouths. They exercise careful judgment with how they speak. They are *slow to speak, quick to hear, and slow to anger* (James 1:19). They've learned to not give voice to every impulse that crosses their mind. They've done the hard work of examining all sides of the issue so they can understand why people feel the way they do. Most of the reconciliation I've attempted to broker between arguing people fails at this point. The facts are presented, the justifications are made, and there may even be agreement concerning what happened by everyone. But when there is no willingness to get in the shoes of the person you're at odds with, there's almost always no real reconciliation. When we refuse to attempt feeling what others feel, we will remain stubbornly entrenched in our points of view, intractable and hard-hearted.

Why? Because it will cost us too much. I recently heard Dr. Paul Tripp say this in a message. "How much of your anger toward the people around you in the last few weeks had anything to do with the kingdom of God? Be honest. You're not typically angry because people are breaking the laws of God's kingdom. You're angry because they're breaking the laws of *your* kingdom. They're in the way of what you want, of what you plant, of what you think is comfortable, of what you think you need... you, you, you, you."[6] Moses had much to lose. He *literally* had a kingdom to lose. He risked it to do the right thing. And he lost it.

Don't be surprised when the call to follow Jesus leads you to loss: loss of respect among men, of income, of authority, of position, of dignity. Remember his teaching.

> For whoever would save his life will lose it, **but whoever loses his life for my sake will find it**. (Matthew 16:25)

What you are about to read isn't going to be easy. It hasn't been easy for me to assimilate these things in my life. And in the spirit of full disclosure, I'm still working on it. But the way God has been dogpiling these things into my heart has brought me to critical mass. I'm either going to do something about it and take a stand, or I'm going to fade into deadly, comfortable, kingdom obscurity. I'm choosing to stand. I'm choosing baptism by fire. I'm choosing the loss of all things. I'm choosing the new man that Jesus is building. I'm choosing resurrection. Because the path of least resistance is always of the flesh and leads to death. Are you ready to swim upstream, against the world, against the powers of darkness, and yes, even against comfortable Christians? Here goes.

References.
1. Aling, Charles. *Egypt and Bible History: From Earliest Times to 1000 BC*, page 106.
2. Jamieson, Fausset, and Brown Commentary. Public Domain.
3. Matt Chandler preached a sermon series through Exodus from August 2016 through May 2017 in which he demonstrated that each plague was a demonstration of God's power over the gods of Egypt. https://www.tvcresources.net/resource-library/sermons/by-series/exodus
4. I read through several commentaries and even some articles on Egyptian customs for weaning children. No exact age is given for Moses when he was given to Pharaoh's daughter, but based on my readings around three years old seems a likely age.
5. The Pulpit Commentary, Electronic Database. Copyright © 2001, 2003, 2005, 2006, 2010. https://biblehub.com/commentaries/pulpit/exodus/2.htm
6. "So You've Been Sinned Against" Dr. Paul Tripp, preached at Epiphany Fellowship, Philadelphia, Pennsylvania, April 22, 2018. Available through Epiphany's podcast.

THE ENEMY OF UNITY

When Moses had that initial thought of standing up for his Hebrew brother who was being beaten by an Egyptian, do you know what was happening? In that moment, he felt a sense of *unity* with the rest of the Hebrew people, even though it had been decades since he lived among them. The feeling of family, the sense of identity, the things that Amram and Jochebed had instilled in him before he was adopted into the royal court, they all flashed through his mind and rushed into his heart, coursing compassion and zeal for this brother through his veins. That sense of unity sparked action – even if Satan perverted it, but we'll get to that later in the book.

It might amuse you to learn that an argument with my wife is what has finally given me the inspiration I need to really get moving on this topic of unity. I'm not going to bore you with the silliness of what we're fighting about. Truthfully, it's probably more my fault than hers. When we disagree, sometimes I overstate the case, and my use of hyperbole (*you always, you never*) doesn't really help me. It only entrenches Radene further into her position as her defenses start rising. It's surprising how we will trade off sweet unity for things like *always being right*. Unity is powerful, and its power makes it a precious commodity. The psalmist says it well:

> Behold, how *good* and *pleasant* it is when brothers dwell in unity! (Psalm 133:1)

How good and pleasant it is when brothers dwell in unity. In the Hebrew, the word for *good* (in this verse) means, *beautiful, best, cheerful, at ease, fair, favor, glad, joyful, kind, precious*.[1] The Hebrew word for *pleasant* means, *delightful, sweet, lovely, agreeable,* and also *singing, sweetly sounding, musical*.[2] Good and pleasant; let's dig into those conditions by making this personal. Would you consider your home a good and pleasant environment? Is your home a place where your friends and family feel secure? I don't mean secure as in safe from intruders, but as in safe from demeaning language; safe from personal attacks; safe from condemnation; safe from language that robs people of life. Are the words spoken in your home useful for encouragement and building up whoever may enter, or are they idle and destructive?

Is your home a place where there is provision? Is there food on the table and money in the bank? But more than that, is there an environment *cultivated* where your family's gifts and talents can be nurtured and developed? Is a culture of trust, built upon honesty and hard work *provided*? Have you ever noticed that *provide* and *divide* have the same root? Provide and divide tend toward opposite definitions. In this case, you can have a home of *provision*, or a home of *division*. Provision multiplies opportunities for growth and harmony. Division cuts in half those opportunities. A home where people are cut down, and are told to lower their expectations for life, is a home of division. A home where the members are encouraged to use their skills and develop their gifts is a home of provision.

Is your home a place of service? (Oh, I know I'm meddling now.) Does everyone in the family share in the responsibilities? Do the children have chores? Does the husband assist his wife with the household and children? Does the wife help her husband with his part? A culture of service doesn't happen naturally. It takes work. It's like shaping a piece of iron on an anvil. But in a good and pleasant home, service isn't just dutiful. It's done out of love for everyone else in the family. The husband serves because he loves his wife, and vice versa. The children pitch in out of love... eventually (I've seen flashes of this in my children, and it's becoming more regular).

Why am I harping on the home? Why am I getting all up in your business about what your household looks like? The home is the incubator for everything in your life. Think about it. Nearly every time there's been a tragic shooting, whether in a school or in a workplace, one of the first things that happens is an investigation into the shooter's home life. Every serial killer ever captured receives a thorough home life examination. We learn so much about the motivations of criminals by just examining the conditions of their homes.

Unity begins at home. If you show me a disgruntled Christian, I'll show you a Christian whose home lacks unity. I've seen it time after time. That

Christian who is consistently stirring the pot, who can't seem to agree with anyone about anything, who always needs to win the argument; it's a sure bet that their home is in disarray. Goodness and pleasantness are fruits of unity. And let me be fair: some of us grew up in chaos, so it *feels* normal. Your family may be in disarray, but you don't recognize it because it's all you've ever known. Disunity has been the norm, so survival has been the game instead of service.

SELFISH AMBITION

Let's cut to the chase. The enemy of all unity is selfish ambition. It is anti-service. It is survival of the fittest. Unity cannot exist in a place where everyone is most concerned about themselves. You'll never find it if you only share the leftovers with everyone in your life. If your family is getting leftover time, leftover attention, leftover love, leftover money, they'll eventually go somewhere else for those things because no one enjoys surviving on leftovers!

One of the trademarks of my wife is that she never wastes food. It's nearly compulsive for her. If we go to a restaurant, we get to-go boxes for the leftovers. If we're at a friend's home for a meal, she gets a little anxious when she sees someone scrape food off their plate into the trash. So you can imagine that our refrigerator is full of leftovers on any given day. And hey, I'm grateful. I've learned that keeping leftovers is actually one of her acts of service for the family. She loves us by making sure that we have food on days when she doesn't have time to cook.

I've learned how to make those leftovers stretch, but after so many days in the fridge, no amount of salt and pepper, and no amount of reheating is going to bring that food back to life. It has decayed to the point that its constituent elements no longer retain the flavor they once had. That's what happens with your leftover time, love, and attention. In a crunch, leftovers can keep things floating. That's what you keep them for. But when your family lives on the leftovers of your selfish ambition, when that's all you give them, eventually the taste is gone; no words, no intentions, no apologies will breathe life back into their hearts. The only thing that will begin to repair that breach is something fresh. A fresh meal. Something that shows you're putting them first and sharing the best of your time, the best of your attention, the best of your love with them.

Selfish ambition always leads us inward. It takes us away from others. And when we do encounter others, we see them as opportunities for advancement; they're stepping stones as the idiom goes. Selfish ambition is rooted in jealousy. When we become jealous of what others have (possessions, relationships, status, etc.), selfish ambition is born, and we pursue what we must to get what they have.

> But if you have bitter jealousy and selfish ambition in your hearts, do not boast and be false to the truth. This is not the wisdom that comes down from above, ***but is earthly, unspiritual, demonic.*** For where jealousy and selfish ambition exist, ***there will be disorder and every vile practice.*** (James 3:14-16)

Look at this. Do you see what I see? Selfish ambition and the jealousy that causes it is earthly, unspiritual, and demonic! Let me make that plain: if you are jealous and filled with selfish ambition, you're being influenced by demons. And wherever there are jealousy and selfish ambition, there will be disorder and every vile practice! That should be no surprise. If you're being influenced by demons, of course your life will be filled with disorder and vile practices. Where there is jealousy, there is selfish ambition. Where there is selfish ambition, there is disorder. Where there is disorder, there is no unity. Where there is no unity, a good and pleasant home is just wishful thinking. Therefore, if your home lacks unity, you'll be grabbing for power, influence, and respect from outside the home in every avenue of your life. Selfish ambition destroys the capacity for unity in the home, and it ripples outward from that epicenter.

Let's define selfish ambition. Ambition itself isn't always a bad thing. Ambition is drive. It's what drives us to make decisions and what puts one foot in front of the other as we journey. I have a desire to write, so I pursue that by blogging, by writing books, by writing occasional newspaper articles, and by keeping a journal. That ambition remains healthy for me as long as it is guided by my desire to help people. My enthusiasm for writing was birthed from my desire to help people understand God's Word. And I'm a better writer than I am a speaker. What I can't communicate clearly verbally, I can in writing. So when you hear me preach, I'm speaking from something that I prayerfully wrote during the preceding week. My strength isn't in impromptu speaking. It's in prayerfully writing down my thoughts and sharing them.

Now, my ambition for writing rides a razor's edge. Along with writing comes influence and a following of people who appreciate what I write. If my reason for writing becomes more about building a platform than helping people, then I will have crossed into selfish ambition. Of course, I want to help as many people as I can, so if my following increases that's not a bad thing, it just sharpens the razor's edge. So our working definition for this chapter will be this: *selfish ambition is ambition that builds your own personal kingdom instead of God's kingdom. It seeks influence and authority to elevate you instead of Jesus Christ.*

Contrast selfish ambition with *godly ambition*. Godly ambition means that everything you do, from providing for your family, to maintaining healthy relationships with your neighbors, to your diligence at work to be punctual and faithful, is done so that when you do open your mouth to share the gospel, there will be no grounds for an accusation against your character. You *make it your ambition* to lead a life that creates no stones of stumbling for anyone as you point them to the cross of Christ for salvation. Christ is himself a stumbling stone (1 Peter 2:8), and that should be the only thing in your life that people trip over. A person with godly ambition will have it said of him or her, "I hate what he believes, but he is my best neighbor." "I despise her Jesus, but she's always there for me in a bind." "What he believes is ludicrous, but he's my best employee." The stumbling stone remains Jesus, not you.

Selfish ambition is a chameleon. It often disguises itself as something pure, something noble, but the ugly reality is that it's really only concerned with self-preservation or self-advancement or both. I've been in ministry for over eighteen years now, and I've seen this first hand in others, but most poignantly in myself. I have to check myself all the time. Is what I'm doing being done for God's kingdom or my kingdom? It's easy to fall into comfort and familiarity with the works that the Lord leads you to do. With comfort and familiarity comes status quo. With status quo comes a desire to maintain. And the desire to maintain the status quo of your life is poisonous to your spiritual journey with Jesus. Selfish ambition puts us in a defensive posture when the status quo is at risk.

A MOTHER'S SCHEME, A HOME DIVIDED

In the book of Genesis, Jacob became poisoned by selfish ambition. Jacob, Isaac's second born, Abraham's grandson, the man who would eventually be renamed

Israel and father twelve sons who would be the progenitors of the Twelve Tribes of Israel, was a selfish man at first. But he didn't become this way in a vacuum. He had some help.

First off, his mother, Rebekah, was troubled.

> And Isaac prayed to the Lord for his wife, because she was barren. And the Lord granted his prayer, and Rebekah his wife conceived. The children struggled together within her, and she said, "If it is thus, why is this happening to me?" So she went to inquire of the Lord. (Genesis 25:21-22)

Rebekah was barren. It says earlier in verse twenty that Isaac didn't marry her until his fortieth year. We don't know how old Rebekah is, but you can safely presume that she is somewhat younger than Isaac. Her barren condition would've been considered a sign of a curse or judgment from the Lord. It says a few verses later that their sons, Esau and Jacob, were born to Isaac when he was sixty years old. The math is simple. Isaac and Rebekah were childless for twenty years. In that twenty years, Isaac and Rebekah prayed and waited. You can imagine their wait was frustrating at times. We can also assume (safely) that during their wait Rebekah bore the reproach for being unable to bear children. The stigma was hers alone, not Isaac's. Today we know better; many times the husband is infertile, but in their day, the blame was laid entirely upon the wife. It's safe to say that Rebekah was troubled.

At last, though, after twenty years of waiting, the Lord answered their prayers. Rebekah conceived. But she didn't conceive a single child, she conceived fraternal twins. Within her were their two sons, Esau and Jacob. And they weren't happy about sharing the small space of their mother's womb. The Bible says *the children struggled together within her.* Even in the womb, these two boys were fighting! It was a sign of things to come. But in the moment, Rebekah only knew that something within her was wrong. So, she inquired of the Lord, and he answered.

> Two nations are in your womb, and two peoples from within you shall be divided; the one shall be stronger than the other, the older shall serve the younger.
> (Genesis 25:23)

Two sons, two prophecies, and one of these prophecies is backward from their custom. *The older shall serve the younger*. This is a culture where the firstborn gets all the blessings. Whichever son was born first would receive a double inheritance. One inheritance is a birthright. Firstborns get the premium inheritance of land, livestock, and wealth. The second inheritance is a blessing. In many cases, the blessing is a prophetic utterance where the father prophesies a blessing over his firstborn son. For the older to serve the younger would be a reversal of the custom. But Rebekah took these things to heart, and because of the Word from the Lord, she favored Jacob.

Jacob's selfish ambition was forged in the passion of his mother's desire to see the Lord's prophecy fulfilled. Esau and Jacob were adversarial. They were two brothers who couldn't be more different. Esau was outdoorsy. Jacob was indoorsy. Isaac favored Esau. Rebekah favored Jacob. This home was divided. Odds are that Rebekah told Isaac about the word she received from the Lord, yet there was no unity. Though both parents knew what the Lord had said, Isaac was determined to bless Esau, and Rebekah was determined to undermine Isaac's intentions. Rebekah instilled in Jacob cunning and craftiness to get what was supposed to be his. And what we see in Jacob is a man willing to cheat, manipulate, and lie to get what he wants. First, Jacob extorted his brother.

> Once when Jacob was cooking stew, Esau came in from the field, and he was exhausted. And Esau said to Jacob, "Let me eat some of that red stew, for I am exhausted!" (Therefore his name was called Edom.) Jacob said, "Sell me your birthright now." Esau said, "I am about to die; of what use is a birthright to me?" Jacob said, "Swear to me now." So he swore to him and sold his birthright to Jacob. Then Jacob gave Esau bread and lentil stew, and he ate and drank and rose and went his way. Thus Esau despised his birthright. (Genesis 25:29-34)

Here's what happened. Jacob knew his brother was immoral and had no regard for his birthright. With that knowledge, he used Esau's birthright as a bargaining chip when Esau was physically weak and emotionally exhausted. He knew his brother would sell out under the right circumstances and pressures. Don't think for a moment that this wasn't a well thought out plan. Jacob was just waiting for his opportunity.

Rebekah's zeal for him to get what belonged to Esau was bearing fruit.

People with selfish ambition plot. They scheme. They manipulate. They're opportunistic. They learn the people they're plotting against and use that knowledge to their advantage. They will even use knowledge of their friends and loved ones when it will benefit them. When the home is divided, as it was in Isaac's, sides are taken, lines are drawn, and opportunities will be exploited to gain the upper hand. But just in case you think I'm being too harsh on Rebekah, her plans are wholly fulfilled when her husband is on his deathbed.

Isaac was afraid he was about to die. He was blind, his health was failing, so he summons Esau. Even now, Isaac is still determined to defy the Lord and give Esau his blessing. Here is where we see Rebekah make her final play to advance Jacob.

> Now Rebekah was listening when Isaac spoke to his son Esau. So when Esau went to the field to hunt for game and bring it, Rebekah said to her son Jacob, "I heard your father speak to your brother Esau, 'Bring me game and prepare for me delicious food, that I may eat it and bless you before the Lord before I die.' Now therefore, my

son, obey my voice as I command you. Go to the flock and bring me two good young goats, so that I may prepare from them delicious food for your father, such as he loves. And you shall bring it to your father to eat, so that he may bless you before he dies."
(Genesis 27:5-10)

And of course, Jacob complies. He goes right along with it, only making objections where he sees weakness in her plan (Genesis 27:11-12). So, Jacob deceives his ailing father with the full support of his mother. And the deception was complete with Isaac's blessing.

> See, the smell of my son is as the smell of a field that the Lord has blessed! May God give you of the dew of heaven and of the fatness of the earth and plenty of grain and wine. Let peoples serve you, and nations bow down to you. Be lord over your brothers, and may your mother's sons bow down to you. Cursed be everyone who curses you, and blessed be everyone who blesses you! (Genesis 27:27-29)

Now, let's examine this. God gave the word, *the older shall serve the younger,* before Esau and Jacob were born. It was a counter-cultural word from God. Isaac was wrong for his obstinance to favor Esau, despite what the Lord said. But Rebekah was also wrong for trying to *make* the Lord's promise come to life by her own cunning and deception. This should sound familiar. Rebekah's father-in-law, Abraham also attempted to *make* the Lord's promise come to life by fathering Ishmael with Hagar instead of waiting on the Lord to give Sarah a child as he had promised (Genesis 16). Any time we try to *make* something happen for the Lord instead of waiting on him to do it, disaster will follow. And often the efforts themselves will cause division and fracture the unity of the home. Whenever we assume control and try to *make* something happen, we are allowing selfish ambition to master us.

What would have happened if Isaac and Rebekah had been unified? What might've been if instead of taking sides, each to their favored son, they just loved their sons equally and let the Lord work in each of their hearts about what he wanted for their lives? If Isaac and Rebekah had kept the Lord's word to them central and sought him instead of pursuing their own desires for their favorites, perhaps God would have persuaded

Esau to surrender his birthright and blessing to Jacob willingly.

But because Isaac was stubborn, Rebekah resorted to deception, Esau saw no value in loving the Lord, Jacob learned to scheme and manipulate, and the end game was Esau's soul was sacrificed on the altar of stubbornness, disunity, and deception. Esau never repented; he never sought the Lord. In fact, the Scripture shows that Esau and all of his descendants – the nation of Edom – never followed the Lord. Take note that the prophet Obadiah's oracle is dedicated to predicting the complete destruction of Edom because they all walked in the same sin of their father, Esau. Two parents, divided, set the course for an entire nation to abandon the Lord and meet destruction.

This brings me to a massive point about unity. Unity is sacrificial. Unity is something that has to be sought. It has to be worked for. You don't just wake up one morning, and suddenly, without effort, your home is in unity. For unity to exist, selfish ambition has to be put to death. If you leave room for selfish ambition in your heart, unity will always be beyond your grasp.

UNITY WITH THE HOLY SPIRIT

Now, let's bring this down to just you. I've been talking a lot about the home and the importance of its unity. But there is a unity that precedes unity in the home. It's a unity that if you don't possess it, the *good* and *pleasant* conditions of Psalm 133 will elude you. Look at the second verse of Psalm 133:

> It is like the *precious oil* on the head, running down on the beard, on the beard of Aaron, running down on the collar of his robes! (Psalm 133:2)

Unity is like *precious oil* on the head, running down on the beard. What does that mean? It certainly isn't talking about the feeling of pouring Wesson over your head: that's terrible. In Israel, kings were anointed with oil. Priests were anointed with oil. This anointing symbolized the arrival of the Holy Spirit. The most vivid example in the Old Testament was the anointing of David.

> Then Samuel took the horn of oil and anointed him in the midst of his brothers. And the Spirit of the LORD

rushed upon David from that day forward. (1 Samuel 16:13)

So, in Psalm 133, *precious oil* tells us that the Holy Spirit is present when we are unified. But not just present, the oil *runs down on the beard*, which is a picture of plenty, abundance, more than enough. So much oil has been poured out that it not only covers the head, but it goes beyond and saturates the beard. When there is unity, the Holy Spirit isn't merely present, he's *abundantly* present. But there's more.

The Psalmist mentions specifically *the beard of Aaron* and that the oil runs down on the *collar of his robes*. The mention of running down on the collar of his robes is another nod to the abundance of the Holy Spirit. There's so much precious oil being poured out that even after saturating the beard, there's still enough to run down on the collar of the robe. PLENTY! But the mention of Aaron has special meaning.

Aaron, the brother of Moses, is the person God chose to be the father of the priestly order (Exodus 28:1-3). He was a Levite, descended from Levi, a son of Israel. Side note: it's a common misconception that all Levites were priests. All priests were indeed Levites, but not all Levites were priests; only the descendants of Aaron were priests. Until Jesus, that is. Jesus fulfills the office of High Priest forever (Hebrews 5:9), effectively nullifying the genealogical requirement of being a descendant of Aaron. Because of this, as believers we become priests – in fact, the Bible calls all believers a nation of priests.

> But you are a chosen race, a *royal priesthood*, a *holy nation*, a people for his own possession, that you may proclaim the excellencies of him who called you out of darkness into his marvelous light. (1 Peter 2:9)

If you are a believer, you are a *priest*. Here's where I've been heading. Psalm 133:2, gives us a picture of unity among God's priests being a Holy Spirit-filled-to-overflowing kind of ordeal. In the Old Testament, that was Aaron and his descendants. Today, post-resurrection, post-Pentecost, that's for every believer, because every believer *is a priest*. Let me make it plain: for believers today, Psalm 133 unity begins with each individual believer being filled to overflowing with the Holy Spirit. I said a few paragraphs ago that there is a unity that precedes unity in the home. Here it is.

There must be unity within before there can be unity without. You must be unified with the Holy Spirit inside before you can foster unity with other people on the outside. Therefore, you have to ask yourself the question: *Am I fighting against the Holy Spirit's work to transform me, or am I fighting alongside the Holy Spirit to transform me?* Would you consider your relationship with the Holy Spirit good and pleasant? Are you submitting to His leadership, or are you continually resisting Him?

There is no doubt that we all experience times of resisting him. That's a given. I'm not talking about the usual resistance that our flesh puts up against the Holy Spirit's work. I'm talking about willful, continuous, consistent, ongoing, unrepentant resistance. Has the Holy Spirit told you to do something that you have consistently refused to do? Have you been avoiding intimacy with God for extended times because you know He has asked you to do something you don't want to do? That's the kind of resistance I'm talking about. If that's you, then you have no internal unity with the Holy Spirit. Real, lasting goodness and pleasantness on the inside simply aren't there. There's no peace. And what you've done to substitute for that peace is run from thing to thing, relationship to relationship, business idea to business idea, ministry to ministry, trying to feel right about your rebellion against the Holy Spirit. If you lack internal unity with the Holy Spirit, you'll lack the stability needed to lead your home into good and pleasant unity.

THE IDOL OF YOUR OPINION

Selfish ambition is an enemy of unity. We've already established that. Stubbornness is too. The heart that is unwilling to follow the Holy Spirit's leadership is poisoned by stubbornness. Here's a very recent example. A while back, I posted a little blurb on Facebook about how we should refrain from complaining against people on public assistance when we see them driving nicer cars or buying better food than we (who have no public assistance) do. I backed it up with Scripture. I mean, it was airtight. And still, there were professing Christians who bristled at what I was saying, and one of them even said that there's something wrong with Christianity. I have no problem being bold about this statement: when you are presented with Scripture that completely refutes your feelings, and you still side with your feelings, you are stubborn.

Beware: stubbornness is *idolatry of your own opinions*.[3] When you resist the Word, when you stiff-arm the Holy Spirit in favor of preserving what you feel is right and just, or what's best for you and your circumstance, you have become an idolater and there will be no internal unity between you and the Holy Spirit until you surrender your worship of your opinions.

I know this very personally. The last couple of years have been difficult, filled with testing and refining. A while back I became involved in trying to help some very dear and close friends reconcile some differences. When they first approached me, I wasn't completely blind to the difficulty that lied ahead, but I completely overestimated my ability to help bring a swift reconciliation. So as this process plodded forward, each step felt like walking through a boggy swamp. I was getting more and more frustrated with my friends. I thought to myself often: *They're all believers, why can't they see what I see? Why can't they understand how Satan is in the midst of this and just rebuke him, forgive each other, reconcile, and move on?* Radene and I have had a lot of pillow talk about this since we became involved. I'm frustrated! She's frustrated! And worse, she and I don't even see eye to eye on a few things in the midst of this. Some of my frustration is with her too! And she's frustrated with me.

Recently, especially as I've been studying this topic of unity, I've been coming to some realizations about my own stubbornness. I've been stubborn with my opinions about how this whole thing needs to shake down. I've been angry because reconciliation has been slower than I thought it should be. I've told the Lord that I give up when he actually hasn't given me permission to give up. I've actively sought ways to excuse myself from this burden through justifications that they're never going to listen. It created some disunity between me and Radene in regard to how we should handle this process.

It created *disunity*. When that finally dawned on my heart, I understood that the disunity which was forming on the outside was a fruit of my disunity with the Holy Spirit on the inside. I've had to surrender my stubbornness. I've had to acknowledge that my ideas about how this should be working out weren't the same as God's ideas. Reconciliation takes time, and it almost always takes more time than we'd like. And those who try to broker reconciliation need more patience than the ones that are being reconciled! You have to possess internal unity with the Holy Spirit before you can foster unity on the outside with other people. In light of that, here's a great question to ask yourself: *Generally speaking, what kind of force are you in your relationships: stabilizing or destabilizing? Do you bring peace, or do you bring division?*

If you're fighting against the Holy Spirit's transforming work, your inner life will lack unity, circumstances will toss you about, and that lack of unity will spill over into every relationship in your life. However, if you're fighting alongside the Holy Spirit *for* your transformation, you'll possess an internal unity with him that provides stability, despite circumstances. And that unity will also spill over into every relationship in your life. Are you starting to see the importance of unity? A good and pleasant relationship with the Holy Spirit enables you to foster good and pleasant relationships in your home, and with others outside your home. Which leads naturally to the final verse of Psalm 133.

UNITY IS STRATEGIC

> It is like the dew of Hermon, which falls on the mountains of Zion! For there the Lord has commanded the blessing, life forevermore. (Psalm 133:3)

Some mountains are mentioned here. Hermon is a mountain in the north of Israel, and the mountains of Zion are referring to the mountains upon which the city of Jerusalem is built. What is the psalmist describing? Unity *is like the dew of Hermon that falls on the mountains of Zion*. Let's talk geography. Hermon and Zion are not in the same geographic area. How does the dew of Hermon, fall on the mountains of Zion? The source of the Jordan River is near the base of Mount Hermon. So, the dew of Hermon falls, collects, and streams into what becomes the Jordan River and flows to Zion. That's a relatively straightforward explanation of what the Psalmist is trying to describe. But what is the relationship between unity and this natural process? Why is unity being compared to this natural occurrence?

Can you handle something a little deeper? I hope so because I'm about to head toward the deep end of the pool. There's more than meets the eye about Mount Hermon. To the ancient Israelites, Mount Hermon was believed to be the place where the events of Genesis 6:1-4 were conceived.[4]

> When man began to multiply on the face of the land and daughters were born to them, the *sons of God* saw that the daughters of man were attractive. And they took as their wives any they chose. Then the Lord said, "My Spirit shall not abide in man forever, for he is flesh: his days

shall be 120 years." *The Nephilim were on the earth in those days, and also afterward, when the sons of God came into the daughters of man, and they bore children to them. These were the mighty men who were of old, the men of renown.* (Genesis 6:1-4)

Now, I don't have enough space in this chapter to dive into in-depth discussions about the sons of God and the Nephilim. I will recommend that you read Michael S. Heiser's book, *The Unseen Realm*, if you want to dig deep into these topics. It is probably the best volume I've ever read that dives into the ramifications of Genesis 6:1-4, how ancient Jews understood it, and the Biblical background behind who the sons of God actually are. Much of what I'm about to say in the next several paragraphs springs from Dr. Heiser's work in *The Unseen Realm*.

First, you need to understand a little of what is called *cosmic geography*. That just means that there are geographic locations that possess spiritual significance in the history of Israel. Mount Hermon and the region of Bashan are not only geographically connected – Bashan is at the southern base of Mount Hermon – but they have a shared spiritual legacy. Deuteronomy 3:1-11 details Bashan and Mount Hermon as part of a larger region that Israel conquered under Moses' leadership.

As I said before, Mount Hermon was widely believed by ancient Israelites to be the location where the sons of God descended from heaven and conspired to mate with human women to conceive the Nephilim. This belief is not found in the Bible, but it is located in the book of 1 Enoch, which while it is not considered Scripture by either Jews or Christians, we know that it was a very prominent book in Jewish theological thinking. It was so influential, that the New Testament authors, Peter and Jude use quotes from 1 Enoch. So, Hermon was considered the place where divine rebels conspired to further corrupt humanity.

Now, take note that Genesis tells us that the Nephilim were the offspring of the sons of God and human women. Also, notice that Genesis informs us that they were on the earth both before the flood and *after the flood*. How did the Nephilim survive the flood? The most coherent answer is that the sons of God continued to reproduce with human women after the flood and produce Nephilim. Where were they after the flood? Note the report of the ten fearful spies who entered the Promised land in Numbers thirteen.

> And there we saw the Nephilim (the sons of Anak, who come from the Nephilim), and we seemed to ourselves like grasshoppers, and so we seemed to them.
> (Numbers 13:33)

You could perhaps make an argument that these fearful spies were lying, but I think not. Later in Deuteronomy three, the Lord led Moses on a mission of conquest in the lands of Sihon and Bashan, east of the Jordan River. When they defeat the king of Bashan, Og, it is said that he was the last of the Rephaim, a clan of giants – a tribe of the Nephilim. In fact, the Scripture even goes as far as to provide the physical dimensions of Og's bed.

> For only Og the king of Bashan was left of the remnant of the Rephaim. Behold, his bed was a bed of iron. Is it not in Rabbah of the Ammonites? Nine cubits was its length, and four cubits its breadth, according to the common cubit. (Deuteronomy 3:11)

The common cubit was about eighteen inches.[5] Therefore, Og's bed was about thirteen and a half feet long by six feet wide. And just in case the ancient reader wanted to see it for himself, he could travel to Rabbah of the Ammonites and see it on display.

So, Og is a Nephilim, ruling over Bashan, at the feet of Mount Hermon. On top of that, Bashan was also called, *the place of the serpent*.[6] If you will recall Psalm 22, David prophesied of Christ's crucifixion in this Psalm, and it says:

> Many bulls encompass me; strong bulls of Bashan surround me; (Psalm 22:12)

This is a reference to the enemies of God. Why are God's enemies specifically from Bashan? Because this place is believed to be *the place of the serpent*. Heiser says, "In effect, Bashan was considered the location of . . . 'the gates of hell.'"[7] In fact, when Jesus said to Peter, "the gates of hell will not prevail," (Matthew 16:13-18) they were in Caesarea Philippi, which was located in the region of Bashan.[8]

And to put the nail in the coffin for this deep dive, the transfiguration of Jesus (Mark 9:2-8) happens on a *high mountain*. The Bible doesn't name the mountain, but it is widely believed that Jesus transfigured on Mount Hermon, the highest peak in Israel. That makes sense. If the sons of God came down to conceive their plan to corrupt humanity on Mount Hermon, it should be no surprise to us that Jesus ascended Mount Hermon to transfigure, and reveal his true nature to Peter, James, and John. His transfiguration on a mountain associated with such wickedness would in effect symbolize the defeat and reversal of the wicked plans that were hatched on the summit of that mountain in the days before the flood.

ALRIGHT! Take a deep breath. I know that for some of you that was a deep dive, and almost too long to hold your breath. Now, let's get back to Psalm 133, unity, and what in the world it has to do with all of what I just said.

> It is like the dew of Hermon, which falls on the mountains of Zion! For there the Lord has commanded the blessing, life forevermore. (Psalm 133:3)

The dew of Hermon; dew is a blessing to any land that it falls upon. It waters the ground, it nourishes the vegetation, it provides a daily drink to the land's inhabitants. Dew, a blessing, even falls upon Hermon, a place of darkness. But the Psalmist says this: unity takes the blessings that fall on the wicked, and sends them to bless God's people. The dew that falls on Hermon flows down the Jordan and blesses God's people in Zion. Let me make it understandable. When God's people dwell together in unity, even the things that bless God's enemies will be turned around to bless God's people. He'll take the dew of Hermon and give water to his own people in Zion. In essence, God takes resources from his enemies, and blesses his people with those resources. If you would, let me rephrase that verse in a way that might help it make more sense.

> Unity is like God taking the dew that nourishes wicked places and sending it to bless his people in Zion. For in Zion, God has promised his blessing of everlasting life. [9]

Let's review. Unity is good and pleasant. It is also both a place where the Holy Spirit is abundant, and something you can't have without the Holy Spirit's presence. And it is a condition where resources from the enemy are taken and used to bless God's people. That leads me to the final enemy of unity: Satan himself.

This shouldn't have been hard to guess, but I did all this footwork to demonstrate how good unity is to God's people and how dangerous it is to Satan and his plans. When a person is internally unified, when his family is unified, and when the Church is unified, that's a triple threat against the schemes of the devil. When Satan's resources are being redirected to God's people, you know it is the fulfillment of Jesus' declaration to Peter, *"on this rock I will build my church, and the gates of hell shall not prevail against it."* (Matthew 16:18)

Unity isn't just a state of affairs among God's people. It is a strategy to do massive damage to the gates of hell. Gates are defensive structures, not offensive weapons. [10] What does that mean? We often think of Hell as being the aggressor. But by Jesus' own words, Hell is a kingdom for the taking. The church must only launch her assault on Hell's gates, *and those gates will not prevail*! Unity is a non-negotiable strategy for assault on the gates of Hell. Without it, we might as well be fighting with pea shooters and spit wads.

So… What is the state of your internal unity? Are you in unity with the Holy Spirit within? How's the unity in your home? Can you call your home a *good* and *pleasant* place? Is your church walking in unity? Is the fellowship of your church also *good* and *pleasant*? Is your church seeking unity with other churches? These are all essential questions that need to be answered. This brand of unity is *supernatural*! It is given by the Holy Spirit. It is also abundantly filled by the Holy Spirit. It takes from the enemy and blesses God's people with the spoils of war. It should be something we pursue with pit bull tenacity… but sadly, we don't. The Father, Yahweh, sent Jesus to die for our unity. Shouldn't we die trying to lay hold of it?

> I do not ask for these only, but also for those who will believe in me through their word, *that they may all be one*, just as you, Father, are in me, and I in you, *that they also may be in us*, so that the world may believe that you have sent me. (John 17:20-21)

References:
1. Strong's number h2896.
2. Strong's number h5273.
3. A quote from Pastor Jimmy Evans' message at the 2017 Gateway Conference.
4. Heiser, The Unseen Realm, page 285.
5. *How Long Was the Original Cubit?* Answers in Genesis. https://answersingenesis.org/noahs-ark/how-long-was-the-original-cubit/
6. Heiser, *The Unseen Realm*, page 200.
7. Heiser, *The Unseen Realm*, page 201.
8. Heiser, *The Unseen Realm*, page 283.
9. My own translation of Psalm 133:3. It is not scholar reviewed, it's just how I understand it best.
10. Heiser, *The Unseen Realm*, page 285.

THE DEVIL'S IN THE DETAILS

I'm no military genius. I've never served in the armed forces so I won't pretend to know anything about military strategy, except what I learn from war documentaries – which I really enjoy – and from history classes – which I don't remember. But I do know this. Great lengths are gone to by governments to learn about their enemies. Spies, satellites, wiretaps, cyber warfare, the list of our efforts to get the intelligence upper hand on our enemies is extensive. Why? If we know their plans, we can prepare countermeasures against those plans. But better than knowing your enemy's plan is to actually *know* your enemy. Understanding the way your enemy thinks, understanding their motives for being at war with you can be more valuable than having a map of their tactical strategies. Knowing your enemy can help you anticipate their next move before it's even on their drawing board. You're not being psychic or anything like that, but instead, you know your enemy so well that you can reasonably predict their next move.

In the Cold War, there was a lot of psychological warfare. What I mean by that is the United States took risks, betting that we knew ahead of time how the Soviets would react. I grew up in the 1980s during the Reagan presidency. He gambled that if we increased our military spending, the Soviets would increase theirs as well – which they couldn't really afford to do. But along with the military spending increase came the legendary Strategic Defense Initiative (SDI) – popularly known as Star Wars. It was touted as a missile shield that would protect America and her allies from all nuclear attacks from the Soviet Union by shooting down their missiles with lasers from orbit.[1]

The truth was SDI was mostly a bluff. We didn't possess the technology to make that happen, nor would we any time soon. Only recently are we starting to see some of that become a reality, thirty-five years after the fact, but at the time, it was total technological bravado and bluster. But the Soviets didn't know that. The gamble was that the Soviet Union would spend themselves into oblivion and collapse their already failing economy trying to counteract the military increases of the United States. And for the most part, that happened. The Soviet Union collapsed, December 25, 1991.[2]

Know your enemy. There's something to be said for the Devil. I think in our efforts to maximize our spiritual journey with Christ, we tend to minimize the Devil. We think too little of him. We speak disparagingly of him. We share silly social media memes that claim reading your Bible gives the Devil a headache. But the truth is that he's a beautiful, powerful, divine creature, created by God to serve a specific purpose among the other sons of God. Yet, his rebellion – the first rebellion – has put him at odds with God and the people of God ever since. In fact, so revered was he among the sons of God, even Michael the archangel would not directly rebuke him, but instead invoked the name of the Lord.

> But when the archangel Michael, contending with the devil, was disputing about the body of Moses, he did not presume to pronounce a blasphemous judgment, but said, "The Lord rebuke you." (Jude 1:9)

Consider this: Moses murdered an Egyptian. It's easy to just say he was angry and move on. Don't simply keep reading, but stop and think. Why did he murder? Remember when Jesus said that Satan was a murderer from the beginning (John 8:44)? All murder is demonic. In that moment of rage, Satan made his move on Moses, and the result was rage that led to murder. The Devil took his opportunity and won the moment with Moses. We are vulnerable to his schemes because we're sinful, broken people.

Toward the end of our discussion in the previous chapter, we identified Satan himself as an enemy of our unity. While that seemed like an obvious answer, based on how we so flippantly speak of the Devil, I'm not sure we take him as seriously as we should. Not to rehash the discussion about unity, but if we actually understood how the Devil's in the details of much of our division, we'd be much wiser, much less prone to escalating the conflict, and much more willing to forgive.

As we continue this journey, I think right now is a good time to actually dive into the topic of our great adversary, Satan. If we don't know our enemy, understand his schemes, and anticipate his moves, we will be caught with our defenses down again and again. So, just for a bit let's dive into the topic of Satan.

ANOINTED GUARDIAN CHERUB

Who is Satan? I don't want to get so basic that I insult your intelligence, but this is actually a question that needs to be asked and answered biblically. There's a great deal of misinformation loose in the Christian subculture about Satan. I've already given you a few answers. Satan was created by Yahweh as a beautiful, powerful, divine creature to serve a specific purpose among the sons of God. So, let's break down those things. One of the best places to read in the Bible about the creation of Satan is in Ezekiel 28.

> You were in Eden, the garden of God; Every precious stone was your covering: The sardius, topaz, and diamond, beryl, onyx, and jasper, sapphire, turquoise, and emerald with gold. The workmanship of your timbrels and pipes was prepared for you on the day you were created. (Ezekiel 28:13, NKJV)

I quoted this from the New King James Version of the Bible to highlight one thing that many other Bible versions do not. First, notice the location. *You were in Eden.* The greater context of this chapter is a Word from the Lord against the King of Tyre, but when God says, "You were in Eden, the garden of God," a double meaning is intended. The fall of the King of Tyre is now being compared to the Fall of Satan himself. So now we're getting a peek into what Satan was like when he was created.

Next, notice the precious stones. Satan was clothed in every precious stone you can think of. In the book of Isaiah – which we'll get to shortly – Satan is described as a light bearer. He's called the Morning Star, son of the Dawn. In fact, the name *Satan* isn't his original name. We don't really know his original name. *Lucifer* is a Latin name translated later from the Hebrew [3], but the Hebrew word used by Isaiah simply means *shining one*.[4] All these stones reflect light, reflect the glory of Yahweh, making him perhaps the most beautiful and brilliant of all the sons of God.

Now notice the workmanship of his *timbrels and pipes*. This is why I chose NKJV for this verse's translation. The ESV says *settings and engravings*. The NIV says *settings and mountings*. Apparently, the Hebrew can be translated to English in a few different ways. *Settings and engravings* or *mountings* have to do with the places where the precious stones are secured in place on the garment. But another way to understand the Hebrew is *timbrels and pipes*. If the NKJV is accurate, then Satan was created with musical instruments built in place.⁵ Not only would he have been a light bearer, but also a musician. You could say that Satan was created to be an instrument and leader of worship among the sons of God. But that's not all. Look at the next verse.

> You were an anointed guardian cherub. I placed you; you were on the holy mountain of God; in the midst of the stones of fire you walked. (Ezekiel 28:14)

Satan was an *anointed guardian cherub*. Let's break that down. Satan was *anointed*. Let's separate that from the churchy way that we like to use that word. Christians are frequently guilty of saying something or someone is *anointed*. Often, what we mean by that is a song or a sermon or a person was used by God to speak into their hearts with a very timely word of encouragement or exhortation. It's a loose way of using the word when you consider what it means in the Bible. To say something is anointed means it's set apart. It means consecrated. Kings would be anointed with oil at the outset of their rule. Prophets would be anointed with oil as a part of their regular ministry in the Temple. To be anointed is to be set apart for a divine purpose. Satan was *set apart* by Yahweh for a specific role.

Next, Satan was a *guardian*. To be a guardian implies strength, authority, and power that have been given to you for that purpose. What was he guarding? Satan was a *cherub*. The *cherubim* (plural of cherub) are divine beings whose main assignment was guarding the throne of God (Psalm 99:1), and the Tree of Life (Genesis 3:24). So, Satan was a member of the cherubim, who were set apart as guardians of God's throne, and later, the Tree of Life after the fall of mankind. If that is too lofty an idea to think about, just think of them as the bouncers of God's kingdom; really beautiful, powerful, divine bouncers who have flaming swords.

Now I know what you're thinking. Why does God's throne need protection? Isn't God all-powerful? The cherubim aren't there for God's protection. They are there to protect everyone else. The time that Moses asked if he could see all of God's glory (Exodus 33:17-23) God basically told him that if you really see my face and all of my splendor, you'll die. The cherubim are there to guard the throne for the sake of those like Moses, who want to see him, but would never survive the encounter. In Isaiah chapter six, even the *seraphim* (a different order of angels) who fly around the throne all day shouting praises to Yahweh have six wings: two for flying, but then two to cover their eyes, and two to cover their feet.

Being in close proximity to God is even hazardous to the angelic host!

THE SPIRITUAL WAR BEGINS

So, what happened? How does a cherub, so perfect, so beautiful, so divine, fall from his station? The only answer is that God has given the angelic order free will, just as he has given mankind free will. And what is free will? It is the ability given to angels and humans to choose whether they will be faithful to Yahweh with glad, loving loyalty. God desires loving loyalty because he desires a family relationship with his creation. He wants glad loyalty because he doesn't want begrudging obedience from his children.[6] Free will gives us the ability to choose this kind of faithfulness to God. It must be a choice, or else it isn't real. Therefore, every angelic order, every human ever created has been given a free will so that when they choose faithfulness to God, it is a real personal choice.

> From the day you were created you were blameless in your ways until wickedness was found in you. Through the abundance of your trade, you were filled with violence, and you sinned. So I expelled you in disgrace

from the mountain of God, and banished you, guardian cherub, from among the fiery stones. (Ezekiel 28:15-16)

Satan's fall came through *the abundance of his trade.* What does that mean? He was an anointed guardian cherub. He was always before the throne of God. He was perhaps even creating the music for the worship that was happening before the throne through is timbrels and pipes. How was he trading? When we think of trading, we think of an exchange of goods. One nation trades with another through exchanging goods and services. Two friends on the playground trade toys because they both have a toy that the other wants. How does Satan do any trading when he is continuously stationed at the throne of God?

Your heart became proud because of your beauty; For the sake of your splendor you corrupted your wisdom. So I threw you down to the ground; I made you a spectacle before kings. (Ezekiel 28:17)

The Prophet Isaiah gives us a little more insight...

> You said to yourself, "I will ascend to the heavens; I will set up my throne above the stars of God. I will sit on the mount of the gods' assembly, in the remotest parts of the North. I will ascend above the highest clouds; I will make myself like the Most High." (Isaiah 14:13-14)

Satan's *trading* was actually something happening in his own heart. He was exchanging worship that belonged to God for his own vanity. He was taking praises that were meant for God and keeping them for himself. Ezekiel says that his heart became proud because of his own beauty. Isaiah says that he began to believe that he deserved the worship that Yahweh was receiving. He began to dream of how he could set up his own throne above the Lord's.

The Lord perceived his heart. I sometimes wonder if this was immediate. Did God make his move to expel Satan at his first thoughts of vanity, or was he merciful and allow Satan time to change his thinking? We can't know for sure, but I'll wager that God gave him some time to change his thinking because God is merciful and slow to anger (Exodus 34:6, Numbers 14:18, Nehemiah 9:31, Psalm 86:5, 15, Joel 2:13). But regardless, Satan did not change his heart. He persisted in his vain thinking, trading his worship for vanity, and God expelled him.

> ...So I expelled you in disgrace from the mountain of God, and banished you, guardian cherub, from among the fiery stones. (Ezekiel 28:16b)

Here's where it gets interesting. In the scenes that we find in Isaiah and Ezekiel, the only one being cast out is Satan. In these passages, there is no indication that anyone else was cast out with him. However, the popular teaching of the Bible says that one-third of the angels fell with him. This is based on how we interpret Revelation 12:3-4.

> Then another sign appeared in heaven: There was a great fiery red dragon having seven heads and ten horns, and on its heads were seven crowns. Its tail swept away *a third of the stars in heaven and hurled them to the earth.* And the dragon stood in front of the woman who was about to give birth, so that when she did give birth it might devour her child.

Traditionally stars are used as metaphors for angels, so many have interpreted that one-third of the angelic host followed Satan in his rebellion. I'm not saying that's incorrect. I actually tend to agree with it, but at the same time, many passages in Revelation are full of imagery and metaphor that aren't always meant to be taken in a very literal sense. So, I don't have a problem with believing a third of the angels followed Satan in his rebellion, but I also don't hold on to that number with a tight grip. All we can say with one hundred percent certainty is that *some* number of the angelic order rebelled *after* Satan became the first and original rebel.

Another interesting point that I want to draw out is the timing of the rebellion. We assume that the entire number of angels who rebelled with Satan all rebelled at the same time. Apart from the vision John records in Revelation 12 – which covers *ages* of spiritual war in only a few words – there is nothing in the Scripture that definitively says this. In fact, you can make an argument that this rebellion happened gradually, and not all at once. Let me show you.

You see Satan in the garden of Eden, tempting Eve. The next mention of any other sons of God is in Genesis 6:1-2.

> When mankind began to multiply on the earth and daughters were born to them, the *sons of God* saw that the daughters of mankind were beautiful, and they took any they chose as wives for themselves.

So here we see that more of the angelic order has fallen. But that's not the only time. Keep reading.

> The Nephilim were on the earth *both in those days and afterward*, when the sons of God came to the daughters of mankind, who bore children to them. They were the powerful men of old, the famous men. (Genesis 6:4)

The Nephilim were the offspring of the sons of God and human women. They were the *powerful men of old, the famous men*. But here it is. They were on the earth both in the days prior and *after the flood*. If the flood destroyed all life, except Noah and his family, then the only way there could have been Nephilim on the earth after the flood is *if more sons of God came down and had children with human women after the deluge.* It could be that there was a gradual fall of other angelic beings after the fall of Satan who were so influenced by him that they later chose to follow him. Or it could also be that they all fell together. Take your pick.

Let me draw out one more thing. Satan was one rebelling divine being. More rebelling divine beings came down later to do further atrocities against humanity. Were Satan and these other rebelling sons of God in cahoots? Perhaps, and perhaps not. So, early in creative history, there is no sign given that the rebelling sons of God were always working from the same playbook.[7] Even throughout the Old Testament, Satan isn't really mentioned all that often. It isn't until the time of Jesus that Satan is identified as the leader of all rebelling spiritual forces. Is that because by Jesus' day there was a better understanding of the unseen realm, or is it because the forces of darkness were kind of chaotic and in disarray until Jesus arrived on the scene? We can't know for sure. I can lean either way, but I tend to lean toward the chaotic and disarrayed narrative for one reason. Confusion, selfish ambition, chaos, lies, and whatever vile practice you can think of are things that we associate with the powers of darkness. I don't think they united to do anything until they saw the Son of God arrive on earth to carry out his ministry. And even then, they didn't understand because if they had known killing Jesus would mean their ultimate defeat, they would've never had him crucified (1 Corinthians 2:8).

Now, take a breather. I just filled your head with a lot of information about Satan. I still have one more thing to say about him before I get to the meat of this chapter, but I don't want you to be worn out. So just for a moment, pause and ask yourself this question. Is what I have always believed about Satan based on Scripture, or based on someone else's ideas, thoughts, and opinions? It is vital that how we think of the Devil be based on what God's Word has revealed about him, not what popular culture or other religions, or even classic literature teaches. Do you realize that many Christians have gotten their ideas about the supernatural realm, including Satan, from John Milton's epic poem, *Paradise Lost*, not the Bible, and don't even realize it?[8] We must become students of the Word of God where the supernatural realm is concerned; otherwise, we'll fall prey to ideas that sound good but aren't true.

LOWER-CASE SON

Allow me to dive into one more thing about Satan. I keep calling him a *son of God*. And I've called other angelic beings *sons of God*. In my defense, the Bible does it first, so I'm just repeating what the Bible says. I need to be clear on something. Jesus, the Son of God, has existed eternally. He is the only *begotten son* of God. I don't usually use the word *begotten* because it's kind of old, but I'm going to use it here to make a point. In the literal sense, to be a begotten son, it means that your father's DNA is a part of who you are. Adopted sons aren't begotten, even though they are loved and treated as begotten sons. When Jesus said in the Gospel of John, *"I and the Father are one,"* (John 10:30) he's speaking of his begotten status. He is the literal reproduction of his Father. He bears within him everything the Father is, and that is something to which only Jesus Christ can lay claim.

But the Bible also speaks of other sons of God, like in Genesis 6. These sons of God were not begotten sons. They were created sons. Later, God calls Israel his *firstborn son* in Exodus 4:22. Then we see in Job 1:6 that Satan was counted among the *sons of God*, even as he had already rebelled. So, leave room for this thought in your heart. When God created the angelic order and humanity, he was creating us all to exist as one divine family. The rebellion of some angels and of humanity has only delayed the ultimate fulfillment of God's purpose in creating us – to be one big family with him.

He created us to be family in the beginning, and in the end we will finally be together as family.

> And I heard a loud voice from the throne saying, "Behold, the dwelling place of God is with man. He will dwell with them, and they will be his people, and God himself will be with them as their God. (Revelation 21:3)

However, we have not reached that final state. Right now, we live in an *in-between* time which means we still must contend with the forces of darkness until they are finally judged and cast away for eternity.

HE TEMPTS, THEN DEVOURS US

So, let's review. Satan is beautiful, powerful, divine, and full of himself, which is why he was cast out. He became the head of all the rebelling sons of God, all demons, and is the agitator of all evil and wickedness on the earth by tempting the flesh of fallen humanity. He led the forces of darkness in their quest to kill Jesus Christ, but in doing so unwittingly sealed their own defeat. Now he is cast down (Revelation 12:9), but not imprisoned, so Peter describes him as a roaring lion who prowls around seeking someone to devour (1 Peter 5:8).

> Be sober-minded; be watchful. Your adversary the devil prowls around like a roaring lion, seeking someone to devour.

Now that we know all of this, what can we do to make ourselves ready? We know that our mortal enemy, Satan, is prowling around seeking to destroy whomever he can. How does our knowledge of him give us a plan which prevents him from taking advantage of us? In 2 Corinthians 2:10-11, Paul says that if the Corinthian church decides to forgive a person, he too would forgive them so that his unity with them might not be broken, giving Satan an advantage to come in and cause further division.

> Anyone you forgive, I do too. For what I have forgiven — if I have forgiven anything — it is for your benefit in the presence of Christ, so that we may not be taken advantage of by Satan. *For we are not ignorant of his schemes.* (2 Corinthians 2:10-11)

One scheme of Satan is to destroy unity among God's people. I dealt with that in the previous chapter but let me give you a real-life example of how I've witnessed unity broken between brothers by falling prey to the Devil's temptations.

We need to deal with problems quickly. One of the biggest lies that Satan tempts us with is that if we leave it alone, it'll take care of itself. And don't get me wrong, I think there is something to be said for how *time heals all wounds*. But a severe wound that is never dressed gets infected, turns gangrenous, and will eventually result in an amputation. Time doesn't heal in that case. Time only causes more sickness with an undressed wound. The way a wound heals with time is if it is dressed and medicated correctly.

Let me tell you about my sister Kelly. In our lives, we had several confrontations, one in particular came to blows. This wasn't my best moment. We were both very young adults; I was twenty, she was nineteen. I'm going to be brutally honest with you. Neither of us had done an outstanding job of honoring our parents over the few years that preceded this. I had been in college, paying little attention to my parents' needs, and she was living at home kind of thumbing her nose at the house rules and doing whatever she wanted to do. But, this particular summer, I was beginning to snap out of it. God was starting to show me how big of a jerk I had been to my parents, so I was hyper-sensitive to *any* disrespect my sisters lobbed toward our parents.

One day I walked in on an argument between her and my mom. My temper went from zero to ninety in a split second. I rushed over, got in her face, commenced to lecture her very loudly about her disrespect, then in the midst of our loud conversation, I was pushed. And before I knew it, almost automatically, my hand swung and slapped her across the face. Then it was on. But not in a barroom brawl way, kind of in a sibling fight kind of way. She swung back, I grabbed her hair, and before we knew it, we moved the fight into the living room where she was in the recliner kicking me in the chest in her best attempt to keep my hands away from her head. Then as quickly as it started, we stopped. We were still mad, but we decided no one was winning, so we ceased fire.

You know what got fixed that day? Nothing. Nada. Zilch. Zero. She continued disrespecting my parents, and I kept getting mad at her. Later that summer I moved to Colorado, and we were separated by twelve hundred miles in the days before everyone owned a mobile phone that could do video chat and Facebook. I never asked her for forgiveness. I swept it under the rug and chalked it up to sibling stuff. And you know what else happened? We were never very close after that. I can't speak for her, but I had days where I felt like we should be reconciled. But, I knew that it would mean dragging up a bunch of garbage that might cause more fights; and the last thing our family needed was more fights.

In April of 2013, I had planned a surprise birthday party for Radene. It was perfect. She had no clue, it went off without a hitch. We had it at a friend's house, out in the middle of nowhere, in a cell phone service black hole. There was no reception unless you stood in very specific places. It was a great evening. Radene was surprised and loved, and that's everything I wanted for her. Later in the evening, I stepped outside for a moment, and as I passed through one of those specific spots of cellphone reception, my phone dinged. I had several missed calls and a voicemail from my mom. I stood in that place where I could get service to hear the message. Kelly was in the hospital and was probably not going to make it.

My heart sank into my shoes. I was in shock for a brief moment, but then my instincts kicked in. I gathered my family, I explained to everyone what was going on, we planned for our daughters to stay with friends, and Radene and I immediately departed for Mississippi. Kelly passed away a few hours after we arrived. The emotions I experienced that night in that hospital room are hard to explain. I stood by her bedside, begging God to give her a second lease on life. At that moment, I knew that I would have given anything to bring her back and have those fights that I feared would happen if we started dealing with things. But, it wasn't to be so.

Satan is clever. He crippled my relationship with Kelly through pride and a false sense of peacekeeping. I didn't want to pursue reconciliation with her because I feared the fighting that might ensue. My ego was that I'm the firstborn, I set the example and tone for our sibling relationships, so I'd rather not do anything that might cause a fight. Now, I deal with regret. Regrets about not fixing things. Regrets about being too concerned about preserving a false sense of peace, when as far as I could tell no real peace actually existed. My only hope is that we will be wholly reconciled when we are reunited with Jesus. But what a shame that I was too proud to seek that reconciliation while she was here. What difference would that have made in both of our lives?

The Devil is in the details. He tempted me. I took the bait. And now I live with the aftermath of the choices that I made after taking those baits. How many of you have divisions in your families that still exist *only* because you have allowed the Devil to have his way in the details? Here's the deal about Satan. He doesn't come to you as a scary, devilish, impish ghoul. If he did you'd never follow him. He doesn't tempt you with easy black and white moral choices. He slowly lures you in, one small temptation at a time. No married couple ever begins their marriage with the intention of having an affair. Affairs happen as one small compromise after another is made because one tiny temptation after another has been offered.

    I have counseled believers who are at odds with family members, with other believers, who know the Scriptures about being reconciled, who know it is their responsibility to make the first move toward reconciling but won't do it. Satan is blinding them. He's convinced them that regardless of what the Word says, they are the ones who've been wronged, and they have no real responsibility to try and see reconciliation happen in their relationships. *Nothing could be further from the truth*, but they have taken the bait that Satan offered them and are now entrenched in their own sense of rightness. Let me be clear. Satan isn't holding them captive. He's merely enabled them to become captives of their own flesh!

And ladies and gentlemen therein is the primary tactic of our enemy. Satan doesn't put us in our chains, he only convinces us that putting them on is the best way to deal with our situations. When I say it like that, it sounds incredibly foolish. That's because *it is*. But the deception present in the temptation appeals to our fallen desires. It appeals to our anger. It romances our lust. It seems profitable to our selfish ambition. It tickles our envy. Then we begin reasoning with our old self – a person we are supposed to consider dead (Romans 6:6-7). Let's be honest. How rational is it to reason with a dead person? Yet, that's exactly what we do every time we take Satan's bait. From that point on, for Satan, it's often a *hands-off* kind of deal. As long as we don't have the wherewithal to keep our flesh from winning the fight, he doesn't need to do much more than whisper suggestions in our ears.

HOW'S YOUR SOBRIETY?

Since Satan deals mostly in subtlety, we need to look back at Peter's admonition. He offers two exhortations that will go a long way in keeping Satan's schemes in check. The first is to *be sober-minded*. In the New Testament, the phrase *sober-minded* and the word *sober* both come from the same Greek word. Strong's defines this word as, *to be sober, to be calm and collected in spirit; to be temperate, dispassionate, circumspect.*[9] Let's think about this definition.

CALM AND COLLECTED IN SPIRIT. You can get drunk on anger. You can get drunk on bitterness. You can get drunk on ANY emotion. We're not supposed to be guided by the emotional reactions we have to trouble. Holy Spirit controlled emotions are the goal.

TEMPERATE. In other words, be a person of mild disposition. Be a person of moderation, not given toward extreme swings of mood or behavior. Give the Holy Spirit leadership of your temperament.

DISPASSIONATE. This means be a rational and impartial person. To possess the ability to separate emotion from fact when examining circumstances. You aren't shaken by your emotions or the emotions of others when judging a situation.

CIRCUMSPECT. Look at every angle of the situations you find yourself in, not just your own vantage point. Circumspect means you walk around the issue, examining all sides before making judgment calls. It's a significant component of testing the spirits.

So, to avoid being devoured by Satan, we must be a sober-minded people. Did you realize that being sober-minded includes everything I just listed? It seems like a tall order, but it's entirely possible for the person who cultivates their relationship with the indwelling Spirit of God. The quickest way to allow Satan to dominate the details of your life is to lose your spiritual sobriety.

Friends let me get more specific with this. The issue of spiritual sobriety can come into play in surprising ways within God's family. Jesus charged us to be wise as serpents and innocent as doves (Matthew 10:16) because the ministry he calls us to will be constantly threatened by wolves. Therefore, we need to be cautious about the voices we listen to for instruction and teaching. Don't accept what anyone says as truth just because they speak with authority on matters (that includes me!). Hold every teacher up to the scrutiny of God's Word because some will try to lead you into extremes. Within the church there are extreme movements that you should be aware of and ready to reject when they come knocking. Satan employs extremes in his playbook.

There are extremes which have arisen within the Charismatic stream of the Church that have gained an enormous platform through their worship ministries. Churches in these movements have abandoned orthodoxy and are holding to teachings *and* practices that go beyond the Word of God. They have lost their spiritual sobriety and have instead chased after mystical experiences that aren't found in Scripture, embraced interpretations of Scripture that have no historical attachment, and have started down a path that has Gnostic roots.[10] Gnosticism was and still is a heresy.

But lest you think I'm singling out Charismatics, there are extremes on the other side of the spectrum as well. Extremists in the Charismatic camp may be getting drunk on mystical experiences, but *extreme cessationists* get drunk on knowledge. A cessationist believes that spiritual gifts have *ceased* in part or all together. Many cessationists agree that the Charismatic *sign gifts* of tongues, miracles, and prophecy have ceased, but believe the rest of the gifts are still distributed for use in the Church by the Holy Spirit. I know this camp. I used to be a member of this camp. But, *extreme cessationists* believe that God doesn't speak to individual believers *at all* because we have the full revelation of God in the Word of God; hence, no further direct communication is necessary. This tends to lead people into a very intellectual, knowledge-based pursuit of knowing God instead of a relational experience with God.

So, on one side you have people drunk on experiences and shunning biblical knowledge and on the other you have people drunk on biblical knowledge and shunning experiences. Both are drunk, neither are spiritually sober. There's a desperate need for God's children to be *sober-minded*. If we lose our spiritual sobriety, we become open to Satan's subtle suggestions, which lead us deeper and deeper down the rabbit hole until we find ourselves in bondage to our own flesh.

The fear of many extreme cessationists is losing control; not losing self-control but losing control of their worlds. Much like the Pharisees, extreme cessationists have reduced devotion to God down to a checklist of commands they must follow to remain morally upright. Since their personal commitment to God is a checklist, so will be their church gatherings. Anything outside of the list will be called out of order and never thought to be from God trying to break into their fellowship.

One of the cries of many who flock to the extreme Charismatic camp is that they don't want to miss out on anything that God has for them. If Satan can tempt you by convincing you that you're missing out on something that God has for you, aren't you falling prey to the same temptation he used on Eve? Isn't that a fear-based pursuit? Eve was afraid she was *missing out* on something that God was holding back from her, so she took Satan's bait, and the rest is history. If you're full of fear, you'll always feel like you're missing out. If you're full of love, you'll be content with what you already have in the Holy Spirit.

I am not a cessationist. I'm more of a Charismatic with a seat belt, so let me say this. Personally, I don't subscribe to the idea that God has withheld anything from us. He gave us *everything* when he gave us the Holy Spirit because Jesus paid for us to have *everything*. If we're not walking in the fullness of what he's given us, it's not because there's something he hasn't provided. It's because we haven't fully surrendered ourselves to his rule in our lives. It's because we're not walking in the light as he is in the light. It's because we haven't applied our hearts to understanding his Word, which helps us know his will. It's always, always, always either something within us that hinders the full manifestation of the Holy Spirit, or it's not the time or season of your life which God has chosen to manifest himself more demonstrably. Be content. Be sober-minded. Don't become drunk neither on the pursuit of experiences nor on knowledge. Don't become drunk on the fear that you're missing something that God has for you nor that you'll lose control of your world. You *must* believe what has already been said.

> His divine power has granted to us *all things* that pertain to life and godliness, through the knowledge of him who called us to his own glory and excellence, by which he has granted to us his precious and very great promises, so that through them you may become partakers of the divine nature, having escaped from the corruption that is in the world because of sinful desire. (2 Peter 1:3-4)

Next, after we become sober-minded, we are to be watchful. You can't really be a good watchman or watchwoman if you're drunk on something. When I was in eighth grade, I was on the junior high basketball team. I'm going to be frank: we were terrible. I think we won one game that year, and then later the team we beat, ended up defeating us. It was a lousy year for Myrtle junior high basketball. Well, in one particular game against one of our rival county schools, Ingomar, a young girl caught my eye. Now, I was no lady's man. I was so full of insecurities I didn't even know how to begin to talk to her. She was on the Ingomar junior high girls basketball team. So I got to watch her during the girls game (girls always played before the boys) and I was utterly hooked, but didn't know what to do.

Later after the boys game had started, I was sitting on the team bench. The last thing I thought would happen, happened. She sat down at the end of our bench by the door and began talking to me. I was sucked in like a tractor beam. I saw nothing else, I forgot where I was, I forgot my name; I mean I'm pretty sure I forgot my name because my coach yelled it about three times before a teammate poked me in the back. I turned around and my coach's icy blue eyes were drilling into me, his face was beet red, and smoke was starting to come out of his ears. I think he was upset with me. I was so drunk on this girl, I couldn't watch the game or hear my coach telling me to get on the floor and sub in for someone. That's why spiritual sobriety is important. You can't watch for Satan's schemes if you're drunk on some other pursuit.

So, what is our move? If we know our enemy, if we are sober-minded and watchful, how should we proceed? When you start letting God open your eyes up to the schemes of the Devil, you'll see him at work everywhere. But he's not at work with big huge orange signs that read *Devil At Work*. He's in the details. He's making subtle moves, whispering quiet thoughts into our minds. He's tempting us to hold on to offenses. He's tempting us to wait for our brother or sister to apologize first. He's affirming our prejudices. In every way that's not obvious to us, he's at work. Satan is patient, like any good fisherman. He's laid out an assortment of baits, he's sitting back and waiting for us to nibble. He only needs to convince us to bite, then we're hooked. It's really very little work for him. The only time he has to increase his game is when we raise ours. The closer we walk with Jesus, the more evident and frontal his attacks become. This is why James could write something as ridiculous as this.

> Count it all joy, my brothers, when you meet trials of various kinds, for you know that the testing of your faith produces steadfastness. (James 1:2)

If the attacks of the enemy are becoming plainly evident in your life, take heart. You've become a problem for him. But if you're simply bound up in your own chains of bondage, you were just an easy fish to lure.

References:
1. http://www.coldwar.org/articles/80s/SDI-StarWars.asp
2. http://www.coldwar.org/articles/90s/fall_of_the_soviet_union.asp
3. Faithlife Study Bible commentary on Isaiah 14:12
4. STRONG'S NUMBER: h1966
5. 2016 Gateway Conference, Session 1, Robert Morris. https://youtu.be/3-i9ObaL5mQ
6. See Deuteronomy 28:47-48 where God requires gladness of heart from his people.
7. Heiser, The Unseen Realm, page 331.
8. Heiser's, The Unseen Realm, makes multiple mentions of the influence of Paradise Lost. Page 12. Page 98, footnote 12. Page 324, footnote 3.
9. STRONG'S NUMBER: g3525
10. Here's a simple article on Gnosticism. https://www.gotquestions.org/Christian-gnosticism.html

JESUS TRUMPS

I'm not a big card player, although I do enjoy an occasional game of Spades or Hearts. It just wasn't something my family grew up doing. Card games were introduced to me in college. So, for a few feverish years, I played cards quite a bit. I never really gambled. I've never been the gambling type. Plus, in college, I didn't have *anything* to bet, so it worked out nicely.

I learned more card games in those three years than I can actually remember how to play at this point. But some concepts carried over between the games. One idea is the *trump card*. Sometimes you'd call it a *wildcard*, but the idea is the same. When you play a trump card, regardless of its numeric value or face, that card beats every card on the table. In some games, you declare the trump or wildcard at the outset, and some games have those cards already set. So, if you say that the trump card is the Two of Diamonds, then it doesn't matter if your opponent lays down the Ace of Spades, if you play this lowly, bejeweled deuce, you still win.

Other games have similar concepts. Monopoly has the *Get Out of Jail Free* card that sets you free from jail, *for free*, no matter how long you've been in there. When you use that card, you're set loose. Regardless of the game, the *trump card* concept is a power play. It advances you in the game whether or not you actually deserve to be advanced.

Can I just make a cheesy segue and get to my point? Jesus Christ *trumps* everything in your life. If you profess to be a Christian, then everything in your life should orbit around Jesus Christ and his plans for you. I don't have space – or desire – to cover everything this touches in one chapter. Instead, I want to zoom in on something so specific, so irritating, so controversial, that you might want to throw this book into the nearest fireplace before you finish this chapter. When this book releases, I might stop checking my e-mail and go radio silent on social media for a while because of the topic I'm about to get into.

What is it? Let me put it in one word: *Privilege*. Jesus trumps your privilege. No one likes being called privileged. I don't like it. You don't like it. Neither of us knows anyone who would embrace the description of privileged. But Lord willing, I'm going to show you that you indeed are privileged, and how that permeates every area of your life without you even perceiving it. Then I'm going to show you how Jesus trumps it, and hopefully show you how to let go of it.

WHAT IS PRIVILEGE?

First things first, let's define privilege. Merriam-Webster defines privilege as *a right or immunity granted as a peculiar benefit, advantage, or favor.*[1] Let me make that simpler. Privilege is something you receive that allows you unearned advantage or favor. There are a few things that get conflated with privilege. Sometimes we mix up privilege with liberty or with rights. Those are not the same. Rights are things guaranteed to all citizens. Liberties are things we enjoy which our rights make possible. Here's an example.

In America, all citizens in good standing have a right to own firearms. This is guaranteed by the Second Amendment of our Constitution. Because the right to bear arms is secured by the Second Amendment, citizens have the liberty to engage in hunting, clay shooting, self-defense, and many other *legal* activities with their guns. But liberties can be suppressed without violating the right to own a firearm. If the government placed a moratorium on all hunting, that isn't a violation of your right to own a gun. It is only a suppression of one of the liberties that the Second Amendment has historically made possible. Do you see the difference? Liberties can be limited or taken away without violating the Constitution. Rights, however, cannot be taken away unless actual changes are made to the Constitution.

Privilege is in a different league. It's not in the same class with rights and liberties. All citizens in good standing benefit from rights and liberties. The distribution of privilege isn't always that equitable. Privilege is often dished out on the basis of economics, race, nationality, social status, and even on the basis of your network of friends and acquaintances. For example, if I got to know the right people, every book I've written could potentially gain a much bigger audience than they've enjoyed so far. Were that to happen, by virtue of the people I connected with, I could receive a benefit – a privilege – that I may or may not deserve. Now that also rests on whether my books are worth a plugged nickel. But there are good authors out there who get very little exposure only because they don't have the right connections.

Is that fair? Getting your work noticed isn't free. You have to spend money to get your work seen by the right people. What if you don't have that money? What if you work hard, but never have the cash flow to pour into promoting your creations on a larger platform? Some people, because they have large social media followings, or because they attend large churches, or because they just know the right people, get a relatively easy ride to success with their content.

That was not some Freudian slip. I'm perfectly content with the reach my books have had. But the example is valid. Some people receive privilege because of x, y, or z without having to ask. Their environment, their circumstances, the people they know, the places they live, all come together to hand them the success that other people – who might be better at their craft – never quite seem to achieve.

Now, I can hear my dad already. *Life isn't fair, son, so shut up that complaining!* I get it. I've been taught all my life to suck it up, put on your *big boy pants*, and keep working. Life isn't going to hand you everything on a silver platter, so be content, and continue providing for your family. And I agree. I'm not waiting around for someone to hand me something I don't deserve. I'm going to work and keep working until the Lord brings me home. That's what we're supposed to do.

But that's not all there is to it. Remember, I'm drilling down to the nitty gritty of why we're all privileged, so this may get uncomfortable. You see, the question beneath the question is, *why are you able to work and provide?* Why are any of us able to get up, go to work, bring home a paycheck, make a house payment, and provide for a family? Apart from being physically capable, it's because we received instruction and had it modeled to us by parents who learned it from their parents, so forth. At some point, someone in your past invested in you and showed you how to take care of business, and that pattern has been handed down from parent to child for generations. It's just how it works.

Now, allow me to drive this point a little further. Not everyone receives that kind of instruction from their parents. Even worse, not everyone grows up with parents! A person who grows up without guidance, or without parents at all, doesn't receive the benefits of the instructions that well-parented children receive. It's automatically *harder* for them to achieve what others can achieve. Of course, it's not impossible because there are plenty of testimonies out there of people who grew up orphaned or grew up with deadbeat parents yet defied the odds and became successful and productive members of society. But you cannot deny that theirs was a more difficult journey than it was for those who grew up with good instruction. If you received good instruction in a stable home, you received a privilege that made the path relatively easier.

I know the immediate objection from many who grew up with good parenting is that their lives were hard too, filled with struggles and difficulties. Of course! That's a given because this world is broken, but just take a moment and consider how you would've endured those same struggles and difficulties as an orphan or as a child with bad parents. Regardless of your struggles along the way, regardless of how hard you have worked, if you grew up with parents who instructed you with wisdom and prepared you to be a provider, you received a privilege that not everyone receives.

So, you're able to work and provide because someone showed you how. But it goes farther than that. You're able to work and provide because you have inherited an economic environment that allows you to have a job. Without the work of prior generations who built the America we now enjoy, the simple idea of having a job might not be as simple. Imagine an America where the economy died decades ago, there's no incentive, there's no reward for hard work, so no one opens businesses, no one creates jobs. That happens in places all over the world. It's only providential that it hasn't occurred here.

You've been shown how to work, you've inherited an economy that's usually favorable to getting a job. And lastly, because you're American, even if you're at the American poverty line, you're still wealthy by global standards. Let's say the only job you can land is an hourly wage job at Subway, making sandwiches. If the best wage you can make is twenty thousand dollars a year after taxes, you're still in the top twenty percent of the wealthiest people in the world, having an income that is five times the global average.[2]

If you live in America, you are privileged. That's notwithstanding any discussions about race, gender, religion, or any other way we've demographically divided ourselves. Just being a citizen here puts you on the top of the global dogpile. If you were born here, all of that has been handed to you by no merit of your own. You had parents who taught you, you had forerunners who built a nation for you, and because of their efforts, even with a lousy wage, you are still five times wealthier than nearly six billion other people on the planet.

PRIVILEGE BREEDS ENTITLEMENT

What does that mean? For most of us, it means that we have a built-in, near undetectable sense of *entitlement*. Don't shut the book, hang on! Think with me. Why do we insist that everyone in America speak English? It's because we don't like being inconvenienced by signs and labels that are in Spanish. It's because we don't like *not* understanding the three other people in the elevator speaking Hindi. So, the sense of entitlement says, *I can't understand what they're saying. This is America. Learn English or go back where you came from.* In other words, you feel *entitled* to understand what everyone around you is saying. See, entitlement is sneaky. It comes in forms that we don't always readily recognize. But the truth is because we're all privileged, we're all smitten with varying degrees of entitlement, whether we realize it or not.

Let's jump into the Word before you start thinking I'm making this up. I have no agenda here except to open your eyes to spiritual reality. Jesus tells what's probably his most controversial parable in

Matthew chapter twenty. Depending on what translation of the Bible you have, this parable is entitled *The Parable of the Vineyard Workers*.

> "For the kingdom of heaven is like a master of a house who went out early in the morning to hire laborers for his vineyard. After agreeing with the laborers for a denarius a day, he sent them into his vineyard. And going out about the third hour he saw others standing idle in the marketplace, and to them he said, 'You go into the vineyard too, and whatever is right I will give you.' So they went. Going out again about the sixth hour and the ninth hour, he did the same. And about the eleventh hour he went out and found others standing. And he said to them, 'Why do you stand here idle all day?' They said to him, 'Because no one has hired us.' He said to them, 'You go into the vineyard too.'" (Matthew 20:1-7)

What's happening here? First of all, this is a *kingdom parable*. Kingdom parables are parables that Jesus used in his teaching to help us understand the nature of God's kingdom. In those parables, Jesus uses earthly themes to draw illustrations of kingdom realities. Here, we have a landowner, the master of a house, his vineyard, and the people he hired to work in his vineyard. All the ingredients of privilege and entitlement are here. First off, you have people who are hired to work. Every few hours, throughout the day, the master walked the city streets and found people who can work for him. These workers automatically benefit from an economy where people can own land and hire people to work that land. That's privilege number one.

Then there's something about the workers themselves. Some of them are out early looking for a job, and some are straggling out pretty late in the day. I don't want to read too much into this, but even among the workers, you have some who are eager and some who are lazy. Look where it says, *"About the eleventh hour he went out and found others **standing**."* At the eleventh hour – for our workday that's like saying around 4:00 pm – the master found some guys just *standing around* (to be fair, he found idle men around the third hour as well). What had they been doing all day? I understand that it's possible they just didn't get picked and were left unemployed. But I don't think that's what's happening here. The master accuses them of being *idle all day*. Then the response is given, *because no one hired us*. That's either the truth or an excuse, and I'm leaning toward excuse. The master *found* these men, which perhaps implies they weren't searching. Here's why I think this.

In that day, there were places you'd gather to get hired if you needed work. I don't know what they were called, but if you were employable, you went to one of these job markets to get employed. The fact that it says the master was walking the streets at the third, sixth, ninth, and eleventh hours of the day means that the men he found weren't at the job market to get hired. It says twice that the men he encountered later in the day were *idle*. Privilege number two is that the master, in his kindness, even hired men who weren't looking for work. These men didn't seek opportunity, it was handed to them.

So, what we have here is a situation where men, even the ones who were seeking opportunity at the first hour of the day, were blessed by no virtue of their own. Things beyond their control were in place to give them work. The eager ones were blessed, and the idle ones were also blessed. Remember, this is a picture of the kingdom. And we're about to see why this is so controversial. I think we can internalize and digest the fact that the master of the vineyard was gracious and even hired people who weren't necessarily looking for work. He simply wants to be a blessing to people because he's good and able to do it. But what comes next is a hard pill to swallow for many.

> "And when evening came, the owner of the vineyard said to his foreman, 'Call the laborers and pay them their wages, beginning with the last, up to the first.' And when those hired about the eleventh hour came, each of them received a denarius. Now when those hired first came, they thought they would receive more, but each of them also received a denarius. And on receiving it they grumbled at the master of the house, saying, 'These last worked only one hour, and you have made them equal to us who have borne the burden of the day and the scorching heat.'" (Matthew 20:8-12)

It's quitting time. The sun is nearly set, daylight is fading, so the master tells his vineyard foreman to gather the workers to receive their wages for the day. To the surprise of everyone, he paid every worker he hired *exactly* the same amount. Now, let's call timeout right here. If that doesn't get under your skin, you're not thinking about this hard enough. The men who worked all day long received the same pay as the men who only worked the final hour. If that seems fair to you, it's clear that you and I didn't grow up with the same values. This *really* bothers me! And I'm willing to bet that it bothers you. Why does it bother us? It's easy: since the workers that worked all day worked longer and harder, they feel, and we feel for them, *entitled* to more than those who barely worked at all.

You have privilege that breeds entitlement. A job was offered, a wage was promised. That's privilege. The work was done and an expectation of more compensation arose among the first workers when the people who worked far less received the same pay they were promised. That's entitlement. This sounds strangely American. And if I may meddle a bit, it sounds strangely conservative American. Here's where the huge rub is about to hit you. The conservative American concept of a meritocracy – where you get compensated according to your merit, according to your hard work, according to your time served in the workforce – is foreign to the kingdom of God. Look at how the master responds to the workers' complaints.

> "But he replied to one of them, 'Friend, I am doing you no wrong. Did you not agree with me for a denarius?

Take what belongs to you and go. I choose to give to this last worker as I give to you. Am I not allowed to do what I choose with what belongs to me? Or do you begrudge my generosity?' So the last will be first, and the first last." (Matthew 20:13-16)

The early workers complained about his fairness, but the master turned their grumble around on them and questioned their fairness to him. He gave them exactly what he promised he would give them; is it fair for them to question his integrity? Is it fair for them to, as Jesus put it, *begrudge his generosity*? What the master is saying to his workers is this. *You got exactly what I promised, but rather than expressing gratitude, you complain, and instead of being impressed at my generosity with people who don't deserve it, you grumble that I'm unjust.* To be unjust would have been to give them less than what they were promised, or nothing at all. What the master did was *generous* not *unjust*. So these entitled workers weren't angry because he was unjust, they were angry because he's generous. God's kingdom is generous, and the spiritual reality is many of his children are so earthly in their thinking that they see his generosity to others as an injustice against themselves.

CONFLICTING CITIZENSHIPS

Breathe deeply. I know that some of you are in a tailspin right now because this challenges your thinking. Some of you have already decided that you don't agree. And some of you agree, but you don't see all the connected dots yet. The question I want you to stop and consider at this point is this. Do my privileges as an earthly citizen – regardless of the nation – create conflict with my citizenship in God's kingdom? This is an important question. I've been talking about American rights, liberties, and the privileges we receive from being born here, but citizens of every nation must answer this question. Every country affords its citizens certain rights, liberties, and privileges that come from being born there. How do they conflict with our heavenly citizenship? What entitlements need to die in us so that we're walking as citizens of God's kingdom before any other citizenship? It's a tricky question because, as we've learned, the Devil's in the details.

I used to work for a construction company. It was my first job when Radene and I were married in 1998. When I was initially hired, it was owned and operated by two men in our church. They were gracious to hire me, a kid who had a hard time building a structurally sound dog house. To this day, that job remains one of the most valuable I ever held. I learned skills that are still helping me today. I didn't appreciate it like that at the time, but today I wouldn't trade those experiences for anything. I enjoyed working for these two men.

Probably a year into the job, one morning one of the owners sat me down and broke some bad news to me. His partner had been embezzling thousands of dollars from their accounts, and their partnership was over. I was shocked. I trusted that guy, and he was stealing the money that was supposed to keep the business floating and pay our paychecks every week. This wasn't just a sin against his partner, it was a sin against every employee in the company. Our livelihoods were now at risk because the future of the company was in danger. Fortunately, the company did not shut down, but what did shut down were some good relationships.

In the months that followed, I watched my boss take a very high road with his former partner. He did not press charges, but instead, he sat down with the church elders and his former partner and sought a solution that would protect the name of Christ in the community. I wish I could say that he received back every penny that was stolen. He didn't. I wish I could say that their relationship was restored. It wasn't. My boss took a risk that he would never get back what was stolen for the sake of keeping the name of Jesus away from public ridicule. And he *never did*.

In the years that followed, I've discussed this with others familiar with the situation. We've talked about how perhaps it should've been handled differently by going to the police, by a lawsuit, and whatever other avenues of justice that could've been pursued. But in the end, we were all a bunch of armchair quarterbacks. Only my boss could hear what the Lord was telling him to do.

In later conversations with him, I'm pretty sure even he had some second thoughts about how he handled things, but in the end, I don't recall ever hearing him say that he misunderstood the Lord. He followed Jesus and didn't get back one penny of what was stolen. But he did gain something that is far more valuable than the money he lost. He had to learn how to forgive. That wouldn't have happened had he pursued legal action, or even if he got every penny back. Forgiveness is a gift that we offer to people who *don't* deserve it. We sure didn't deserve it from God, so we too must offer it to people who don't deserve it. My boss was entitled, *justifiably*, to repayment, but the Lord had something better than repayment in mind.

Kingdom living kills entitlement. Jesus trumps your privilege. Regardless of what this world tells you you're entitled to receive, Jesus trumps it. Since Jesus has taught us to take a higher path, as his disciples, we must strive for that higher path. Look at what Paul says to the believers in Corinth.

> To have lawsuits at all with one another is already a defeat for you. *Why not rather suffer wrong? Why not rather be defrauded?* (1 Corinthians 6:7)

Hear me. There is a time to go to law. Paul isn't advocating that all lawsuits are bad, but the kind of suits the Corinthians were pursuing were a black eye on the name of Christ. To keep it simple, Paul is scolding believers for their appearances on Judge Judy. Brother taking brother to court for small claims. *His fence is on my property. Her dog keeps urinating in my flower bed. Their children keep walking on my lawn.* I don't want to trivialize it too much, but the things they were going to court over were issues with which Christian brothers should never darken the doors of a secular courtroom.

Why not suffer wrong? Why not rather be defrauded? Kingdom citizenship doesn't mean we become carpets for everyone to walk on, but it does mean that we are going to protect the name of Jesus before we protect our own interests. Pursue peace and reconciliation with your brother *within the church,* not outside in a worldly courtroom. Bottom line: it is better to be wronged and defrauded than to bring shame on the name of Jesus Christ in the public eye.

Here is where Satan makes his play every time. He tempts our sense of entitlement. *You deserve better than this. You don't deserve to be spoken to like that. You don't deserve to be treated this way.* And if we don't get wise to his schemes, we'll fall for them every time. And on top of that, everything in the world will tell you that you're taking the right course of action. Friends, we are already primed to believe the best about ourselves, our intentions, our motives, and when we're sinned against we don't need much help in thinking we are entitled to justice.

Like I've said previously, I deal with believers – all the time – who are waiting for someone to apologize to them; who are waiting for someone to make the first move in reconciling; who are waiting for someone else to … fill in the blank. In essence, they're waiting for someone else to come and make their lives better. Why is it someone else's responsibility to improve your life? That's entitlement! Instead of waiting around for an apology, Jesus says, get off your hurt feelings and go start the process of making things right again with your brother. Jesus trumps your feelings of entitlement!

> If your brother sins against you, *go and tell him his fault*, between you and him alone. If he listens to you, you have gained your brother. (Matthew 18:15)

ENTITLEMENT RUNS DEEP

But it's not just in our interpersonal relationships. The sense of entitlement spreads its tentacles into every area of life. As Americans, we have First Amendment rights that guarantee our freedom to speak freely. As citizens of God's kingdom, you don't have freedom of speech. But we allow our earthly entitlement to take precedent all the time. As a U.S. citizen, I can say pretty much whatever I want to say, but as a citizen of God's kingdom, I censor my lips to *not* say things that would cause others to stumble over my speech.

Let no corrupting talk come out of your mouths, but only such as is good for building up, as fits the occasion, that it may give grace to those who hear. (Ephesians 4:29)

And whatever you do, *in word* or deed, do everything in the name of the Lord Jesus, giving thanks to God the Father through him. (Colossians 3:17)

but no human being can tame the tongue. It is a restless evil, full of deadly poison. With it we bless our Lord and Father, and with it we curse people who are made in the likeness of God. From the same mouth come blessing and cursing. My brothers, *these things ought not to be so.* (James 3:8-10)

Let's get practical about this. In America, as a white Christian, you're entitled to whatever opinion you want to have about Confederate flags, Confederate statues, the Civil War, slavery, and racism, but if your words about these things cause a black person to stumble away from Christ, *you will be held responsible.* Or maybe you're on the other side of this as a black, American Christian, railing against the sins of white people. If you push a white person away from Christ with your words, *you will be held responsible.* In other news, you can have political opinions and post name-calling, mean-spirited things on social media (conservatives and liberals both do it), but if your words push someone away from Christ, *you will be held responsible.* Citizens of God's kingdom are charged with a higher calling when it comes to our speech – and a stricter judgment!

> I tell you, on the day of judgment people will give account for *every careless word they speak*, for by your words you will be justified, and by your words you will be condemned. (Matthew 12:36)

Jesus' disciples can't just open mouth and let the words fly. We are instructed to consider our words and how they will affect the people who hear them. That's not the American way (even though it should be). The American way is to say what you will and whoever hears it… well, if the shoe fits, wear it. Satan tempts our entitlement. *Say whatever you want, this is America! If it hurts their feelings, it's too bad, truth hurts. You're not going to feel better until you get this off your chest.* But it's all a lie, designed to lure you toward words that kill, not words that give life. Regardless of your rights, your privilege, or your feelings of entitlement, Jesus trumps your right to say whatever you want. Kingdom people are to speak words that encourage, edify, exhort, and bring light. Even when the truth might hurt – and it often does – we maintain an attitude of humility and kindness.

> Now the works of the flesh are evident: sexual immorality, impurity, sensuality, idolatry, sorcery, *enmity, strife, jealousy, fits of anger, rivalries, dissensions, divisions,* envy, drunkenness, orgies, and things like these. I warn you, as I warned you before, that those who do such things will not inherit the kingdom of God. But the fruit of the Spirit is *love, joy, peace, patience, kindness, goodness, faithfulness, gentleness, self-control*; against such things there is no law. *And those who belong to Christ Jesus have crucified the flesh with its passions and desires.* (Galatians 5:19-24)

I italicized the works of the flesh that could be linked to the careless words of a loose tongue. I did the same to all of the aspects of the fruit of the Spirit that are helpful in bridling your tongue; which turns out to be *all of them*. But most importantly, I italicized the reason this is important: because those who belong to Jesus Christ have killed the desires to speak things that lead to *enmity, strife, jealousy, fits of anger, rivalries, dissensions, and divisions*. Jesus trumps our privilege to say whatever we want. He didn't die on the cross so we could say insensitive things that drive people away from him. He paid for our *gentle* response. He paid for our *kind* words. He paid for our *self-controlled* conversations. In light of Jesus' sacrifice, why wouldn't we pursue those things when asked?

    Talk about the schemes of the devil? This one is the most widespread and most unacknowledged scheme that I can see in at work in the Church. Tempt the sense of privilege and entitlement a little bit to tip the believer toward a worldly response, and let that spark burn down the whole house. And the tragic thing is unless you have enough self-awareness to see your privilege, you'll blame someone else for the damage instead of taking responsibility for your own role.

    I said it once already: I have no agenda except to open your eyes to spiritual reality. Of all the chapters in this book, this one is among the hardest to digest. I acknowledge that because it's hard for me. I wrestle with the Parable of the Vineyard Workers. I've got too much earthly thinking in my mind that needs to be renewed. And while I believe the parable clearly teaches that God is generous to people who don't deserve it, elsewhere in the Scripture, God also tells lazy believers that if you don't work, you won't get to eat either (2 Thessalonians 3:10). So there is a balance to strike, but because of sin we are *always* more ready to criticize than to empathize.

Moses had to give up his privilege as an Egyptian royal. His royal status gave him rights, liberties, and privileges that no other Hebrew could ever know. Enter the Devil. *Moses, you can be the rescuer of your people. You can handle this. Kill that Egyptian. You're a royal. No one will ever know.* What was a good idea – to stand up to oppression – was perverted by temptation. Satan tempted Moses' royal entitlements, which led Moses to murder.

JESUS DENIED HIS PRIVILEGE & ENTITLEMENT

There was another temptation of privilege and entitlement, similar to Moses', that happened about two thousand years later.

And the tempter came and said to him, "If you are the Son of God, command these stones to become loaves of bread." (Matthew 4:3)

Then the devil took him to the holy city and set him on the pinnacle of the temple and said to him, "If you are the Son of God, throw yourself down, for it is written, 'He will command his angels concerning you,' and 'On their hands they will bear you up, lest you strike your foot against a stone.'" (Matthew 4:5-6)

Again, the devil took him to a very high mountain and showed him all the kingdoms of the world and their glory. And he said to him, "All these I will give you, if you will fall down and worship me." (Matthew 4:8)

Jesus had privilege. He's the only begotten Son of Yahweh, a member of the Godhead. He is Yahweh in the flesh. Jesus also had entitlement. He rightfully owns every square inch of all creation because he created it! In his case, the entitlement wasn't undue, it was entirely justified and reasonable. So Christ laid down his privilege and entitlement to come to earth, be born of

Mary, and live among us. The King of kings and Lord of lords came down to our level, lived in poverty, learned a trade, and made a meager living as a carpenter before he began his ministry.

Here, at the start of his ministry, Jesus fasts for forty days in the desert, and toward the end of that fast, Satan comes to him and tempts him with privilege. He has the power to change stones into bread to satisfy his hunger. He knows that if his life were to be endangered that angels stand ready to rescue him. These were temptations of his privilege as the Son of Yahweh. He had power and position that afforded him privilege which could make his life easier. But on both counts, Jesus rebuked the Devil.

> But he answered, "It is written, 'Man shall not live by bread alone, but by every word that comes from the mouth of God.'" (Matthew 4:4)

> Jesus said to him, "Again it is written, 'You shall not put the Lord your God to the test.'" (Matthew 4:7)

But the final temptation wasn't at his privilege. It was at his entitlement. Jesus *is* entitled to all the kingdoms of the world and their glory. And even in this truth, Jesus rebukes the Devil again.

> Then Jesus said to him, "Be gone, Satan! For it is written, 'You shall worship the Lord your God and him only shall you serve.'" (Matthew 4:10)

Do you recall why Satan fell from his position in the first place? He was keeping some of the worship of Yahweh for himself. So he agreed to give Jesus all the kingdoms of the earth in exchange for one act of worship! Can you hear the desperation in Satan's voice? He desperately wants God to give him worship. He desperately wants the Creator to worship the created. And his bargaining chip is something he doesn't even own to begin with. Jesus created everything; his name is already on the title deed. So, his best move is to tempt Jesus with something he already owns but hasn't received yet. *Perhaps he'll take the bait. Perhaps he'll fall for the ruse and give me the worship I've wanted for ages.*

Jesus knew that he was entitled to those nations, yet, he laid down his entitlement and set his face toward the cross. At that moment, he could have given in to his rightful entitlement, and traded a little worship for all the kingdoms of the world, *right now*. In fact, he knew that at any moment he could *rightfully* stake his claim to the earth, send Satan to his final doom, and usher in the fully realized kingdom of God. But if he did that it would defeat his purpose for coming. He came to put his people *first*. His people, throughout the ages, would depend on his death on the cross for the forgiveness of their sins. Only then could God have the family he desired to have, with humanity redeemed and reconciled to him as sons and daughters in a kingdom that will never end, and in a creation that will never again suffer death or decay.

> …looking to Jesus, the founder and perfecter of our faith, who *for the joy that was set before him* endured the cross, despising the shame, and is seated at the right hand of the throne of God. (Hebrews 12:2)

Why do we cling so tightly to our privileges and entitlements when Jesus so freely laid his aside for our sakes? Why won't you lay down your privilege and sense of entitlement for the sake of those who the *god of this world* has blinded (2 Corinthians 4:4)? Why do we risk so flippantly causing others to stumble away from Christ because we feel like we have *rights* to say what we think? Why do we think we have rights at all? Jesus laid down *everything* so that you and I might live. Will you lay down everything – your rights, your liberties, your privilege, your sense of entitlement – so that someone else might find life? Jesus did. And we should say, *so will I.*

References:
1. https://www.merriam-webster.com/dictionary/privilege
2. https://www.givingwhatwecan.org/get-involved/how-rich-am-i/

SEEDS OF RECONCILIATION

I'm not sure if there's a more appropriate topic in today's cultural and political climate than *reconciliation*. We are more polarized than ever before. Everyone has retreated into their tribes, into their ideologies, into their ethnicities, and circled the wagons to defend against intrusions. Even in the Church, we've become more tribe oriented. Calvinists, Armenians, Evangelicals, Charismatics, black church, white church, social justice church, fundamental church; where does the polarization stop? For sure, I'm *not* talking about an ecumenical embrace for the sake of an emotional, fuzzy feeling of *can't we all just get along*. We don't have to lay down our theological distinctives on the altar of unity unless those distinctives aren't Biblical. But even so, we can disagree on some things, and still work together.

Several years ago, I was made aware of a series of documents circulating among west Tennessee Southern Baptists called, *How to Smoke Out A Calvinist*.[1] This was really discouraging to me. Thankfully it wasn't coming from denomination officials, but instead from congregation members within the churches who had obtained the documents from seminars which had been held locally.

Being a guy who once considered himself a Calvinist – I don't necessarily theologically identify that way anymore – this kind of hit close to home. I've been in ministry for a long time, but even when I was more dogmatic for John Calvin's understanding of grace, I never felt I was never pushy about it. I was happy to worship alongside my brothers and sisters who saw things differently, and I didn't feel compelled to convert them to my particular way of understanding the Scripture. But when I read these documents, I felt attacked, and I took up some offense for my brothers in Tennessee who believed the way I did.

Thankfully, at that moment in my life, God had already been doing some transforming. I shunned the desire to hop on my blog and raze these unreformed brothers for their ignorance. (I mean, what else could I do? I don't actually live in Tennessee.) Instead, I took a moment to look back on my ministry experiences in the five or six years prior. I asked the question: *Is there anything I've taught, any way I've presented, or any attitude I have held about other people's beliefs that could have created an offense?*

Friends, if you had asked me that question before I read those documents, I would have immediately said *no*. It wasn't even on my radar that I might have possibly been too pushy, or too insistent about how I understood the Bible. But after I read them, and as I processed the wound that they created in me, it slowly began to dawn on me. In some ways, I *had been* that straw man that they were tearing down. Perhaps chalk it up to youthful arrogance that I didn't see it because much of this time in my life was my late twenties and early thirties when I felt like I had so much of the world figured out.

Isn't that how *everyone* is? Republicans have it all figured out. Democrats have it all figured out. Evangelicals have it all figured out. Charismatics have it all figured out. And because we have it all figured out, we don't bother with examining ourselves, and we certainly don't bother to check on the people who are drowning in the wakes of our *vessels of truth*. This is why we're polarized. And I'm here to tell you this: polarization is one of Satan's weapons. If he can get us wrapped up in the rightness of our beliefs, he's got us halfway there. I say *halfway* because there's actually nothing wrong with believing you're correct. Correctness, or confidence in your correctness, isn't the sin itself. The sin comes from disregard or disdain (or both) for people who don't agree with you.

At times it isn't even disregard or disdain. I've spoken with people on things like racism and racial prejudice who I wouldn't consider racist or racially prejudiced people, but their response was essentially indifferent; *I already know what I believe about racism and racial prejudice,* and there was no desire to go any further on the topic. Indifference is just as deadly as disregard and disdain. Disregard says, *your opinion doesn't matter.* Disdain says, *I'm better than you.* Indifference says, *your struggle doesn't bother me.* All of these are patently unchristian responses and should be in the process of being sanctified *out* of our thinking.

To identify with his Hebrew brothers, Moses had to arrest any feelings of disregard, disdain, or indifference that his Egyptian family may have taught him to keep. *As long as they do their work, who cares about the Hebrews? They're slaves, they're going to grumble and complain! You're a royal. Their problems are beneath you. Their struggle isn't your concern.* Disregard, disdain, and indifference lead us to treat people as a means to an end, not as individuals created in the image of God who deserve our respect. If Moses had embraced the royal attitude toward the Hebrews, the only time he would've paid them any mind is when they weren't performing their work, or when they got out of line with disrespect. But because he rejected the privilege and entitlement of the royal family, he was able to continue seeing the Hebrews as family and people deserving of compassion and empathy.

The same can be said of Jesus. He set aside royal status, royal privilege, and royal entitlement so that he could embrace us as family. He had to endure being lowered and debased so that we could find forgiveness through him and entrance into the only royal family that really matters: the family of Yahweh. Because of how Jesus lowered himself, we too must lower ourselves, not think too highly of our opinions and beliefs about others, and engage in basic, loving service to the people who cross paths with us.

THE MINISTRY OF RECONCILIATION

What then will it take to do this? How can we start being agents of reconciliation, and not polarization?

Let's consider what the New Testament says and build from there.

> For if while we were enemies we were *reconciled* to God by the death of his Son, much more, now that we are *reconciled*, shall we be saved by his life. More than that, we also rejoice in God through our Lord Jesus Christ, through whom we have now received *reconciliation*. (Romans 5:10-11)

> Therefore, if anyone is in Christ, he is a new creation. The old has passed away; behold, the new has come. All this is from God, who through Christ *reconciled* us to himself and gave us the ministry of *reconciliation*; that is, in Christ God was *reconciling* the world to himself, not counting their trespasses against them, and entrusting to us the message of *reconciliation*. (2 Corinthians 5:17-19)

To be honest, I'm sitting here, sipping coffee, listening to music that helps my creative process, and I can't find a mooring to anchor me on this topic. Reconciliation is a profound concept, and frankly, the

Lord has been blowing me away lately with how relevant and necessary it is for his Church at this moment. What does it mean to be reconciled to God? Like many believers, I have read this word for decades, and it just passes through like every other word... *reconciled, ok I know what that means, keep going.* Yes, I know the definition, but the ramifications, the effects, the process, the struggle, the emotional stretching, the pain that must be endured to get the outcome of reconciliation isn't communicated in the definition.

What did God endure as he reconciled himself to us? I know that God is all-knowing, all-powerful, and knows the beginning from the end, so nothing takes him by surprise or catches him off guard; he takes no risks because one of the perks that come along with knowing everything is zero possibility of failure. But bear with me for a moment and engage in a little sanctified imagination. Understanding all the theological meaning of God's *omniscience* [2], *omnipotence* [3], *omnipresence* [4], and his *immutability* [5] is one thing, but we tend to favor those things over other realities about God. God has feelings. God has joy. God can be grieved. God can be made angry. God can be made glad. God is even a singer (Zephaniah 3:17), and singing is a *musical expression* of emotions! He experiences these emotions, *even as he knows every outcome and every decision* that men and women will make. Knowing the future doesn't insulate God from having emotional responses to our choices. You know what that means? *God is far more connected to his emotions than you and I ever have been!*

For a moment, pretend that you could know the future of every moment of your life, from this point forward. I don't know about you, but if I had that kind of knowledge – the dates and times of the deaths of my family, the sicknesses we'll endure, the tragedies we'll face, even the victories we'd have – I would be so calloused by it, by the time those events arrived I may not shed a tear. And that's because human beings usually try to protect themselves from hurt. If you know something is coming, you brace yourself, you build walls, you erect defenses that will minimize your pain, if not alleviate it altogether.

That's not so with God. He is always moved to healthy expressions of emotions, even though he's known all along how things would turn out. He's far more emotional, far more connected to his feelings, and far more in control of them than you and I can *ever* imagine in our current state of being. Why is this important? Because reconciliation is an emotional affair.

Imagine the pain of the Father, knowing that his Son would ultimately have to endure an excruciatingly agonizing death in order to make things right. Imagine the dread in the heart of the Son knowing the pain that he was going to suffer. In fact, we don't have to imagine that because the Gospels are very clear about the travail he went through in the hours leading to his arrest in the Garden of Gethsemane. He was so anguished that his sweat became bloody, and he actually for a split second begged the Father to search his infinite wisdom for an alternative path to finish the mission of redemption.

> And he withdrew from them about a stone's throw, and knelt down and prayed, saying, *"Father, if you are willing, remove this cup from me.* Nevertheless, not my will, but yours, be done." And there appeared to him an angel from heaven, strengthening him. And being in an agony he prayed more earnestly; *and his sweat became like great drops of blood* falling down to the ground.
> (Luke 22:41-44)

The high cost of reconciliation made it emotional. So emotional, that the Father dispatched an angel to Gethsemane to encourage and strengthen Jesus in his moment of ultimate human weakness (Luke 22:43). Now, consider this: the Holy Spirit still gets emotional about it. Ephesians chapter four teaches that believers should not *grieve* the Holy Spirit. When we disrespect the price of our redemption with deliberate sin and rebellion the Spirit of God is grieved – made sad – because our redemption cost Jesus his life!

> And do not *grieve* the Holy Spirit of God, by whom you were sealed for the day of redemption. (Ephesians 4:30)

Here is where people disconnect. For Jesus, reconciliation wasn't really a risk. He knew what the outcome was going to be, so he pressed through the emotions, through the pain, took the cross, the Father raised him from death, fifty days later Jesus sent the Holy Spirit, and mission accomplished. Reconciliation between God and man was completed. For people, trying to reconcile with others isn't such a sure thing, so we enter into risk analysis because we do our best to do damage control on emotional pain before we ever start. *If I enter into reconciliation with my brother, what will it cost me?* Let me be clear about two things: it isn't *optional*, and it *will* cost you something.

RECONCILIATION ISN'T OPTIONAL

First, let me show you something in the Bible that will help you see that reconciliation is never optional.

> Therefore, if anyone is in Christ, he is a new creation. The old has passed away; behold, the new has come. *All this is from God, who through Christ reconciled us to himself and gave us the ministry of reconciliation*; that is, in Christ God was reconciling the world to himself, not counting their trespasses against them, and entrusting to us the message of reconciliation. Therefore, we are ambassadors for Christ, God making his appeal through us. We implore you on behalf of Christ, be reconciled to God. For our sake he made him to be sin who knew no sin, so that in him we might become the righteousness of God. (2 Corinthians 5:17-21)

I included the several amazing verses that surround verse eighteen (which is italicized) because they demonstrate the non-optional nature of reconciliation. First of all, as a believer in Christ, you are a *new creation*. You know what that means? That means you can't fall back on the old saying, *I'm not wired that way*. You can no longer say that you were born shy, or you've always had an anger problem, or you've never been good at dealing with emotional things. *You are a new creation!* Either you believe that, or you don't. And if you believe it, then you must believe that your old wiring, your old nature, *has passed away*. Even if you still feel the same old urges for fight or flight, or whatever, part of your sanctification journey is believing, reckoning, living as if that part of you is *dead* (Romans 6:11). Which means, instead of fight or flight, you pursue the third option that Christ has given us: *reconcile*.

Now, you may be thinking, as I once did, that when it says he's given us the ministry of reconciliation, it's talking about spreading the message of the Gospel; that God has reconciled the world to himself, through Christ. That is definitely there, but it's a shallow reading of the passage if your understanding stops there.

Think about it: who does the reconciling? God does. We don't reconcile anyone to God. Jesus did that work on the cross. The task of reconciling people to God has been entirely accomplished by Jesus. So what does it mean when it says that God has now given the ministry of reconciliation to us? We spread the good news of Jesus for sure, but being recipients of the ministry of reconciliation means that we too have become *reconcilers*. And since reconciliation between God and people is already accomplished, there's really only one other realm of relationships that needs reconciling: people to people.

So, we share the Gospel, announcing the good news, imploring people to listen, and through us, God makes his appeal to the nations that through Christ, men can be reconciled to him. That's the *declaration* of reconciliation. But the power of reconciliation is demonstrated in our human relationships. A message without a demonstration of power is nothing more than a plausible argument; one among thousands of other plausible arguments. Paul makes it very clear:

> and my speech and my message were not in *plausible* words of wisdom, but in demonstration of the Spirit and of power, (1 Corinthians 2:4)

> For the kingdom of God does not consist in talk but in power. (1 Corinthians 4:20)

Reconciliation in our human relationships is one very tangible way that God demonstrates the power of the Gospel to the nations. If you call yourself a Christian, but you've let relationships wither on the vine from your own need to always be right, or from your own fear of the emotional cost – fight or flight – then you sir, ma'am, are a walking, talking *plausible argument* for Jesus. There's nothing definite, nothing concrete, nothing for sure about your testimony, except that you *say* that you believe in Jesus and that God has forgiven your sins. You might even live an otherwise moral life, but morality is no indicator of salvation. There are highly moral but spiritually dead people all over this globe. Ever since the birth of the Church, the best evidence for the Holy Spirit's power in a believer's life hasn't rested in morality, it hasn't even rested in the use of spiritual gifts, but it has rested in the ongoing ministry of being a *reconciler*. It's the two-fold ministry of *declaration* and *demonstration* of reconciliation that marks believers as the genuine article. If you're not a reconciler, you don't have any ongoing, real-life evidence that you're a Christian. I'm not being mean, I'm just repeating what the Scripture has already said. You're a plausible argument for Jesus, but not a concrete one.

> So also faith by itself, *if it does not have works*, is dead. But someone will say, "You have faith and I have works."

Show me your faith apart from your works, and I will show you my faith by my works. (James 2:17-18)

It goes on to say that because we've been given the ministry of reconciliation that we are *ambassadors* of Christ. I've mentioned this before in other teachings I've given, and I'll say it here too. Because you're an ambassador, that makes your home an *embassy*. An embassy is a place of refuge on foreign soil. If I were to visit Moscow, Russia and were I to find myself in the wrong place at the wrong time and get accused of a crime that I did not commit, I could contact the American embassy, and they would work to extract me from the Russian authorities. Once I was retrieved and brought to the American embassy, I would be safe from the Russians. Even though the American embassy is on Russian soil, everything within the walls of the embassy is considered American soil. Therefore, anyone who stands within the walls of the American embassy in Moscow, Russia, is afforded the same liberty, rights, and protections as any citizen standing in Washington, D.C. In the eyes of the government, the embassy is sovereign American territory, and any attack on the embassy is an attack on the nation.

As an ambassador for Christ, your home is sovereign Kingdom territory. Reconciliation, therefore, starts in your home. Your home should be marked by relationships that are *always* reconciling. And let's be honest; family relationships are the ones that need the most tender, loving care because we are at our best and our worst with the people who live with us in our embassies. If your family isn't a reconciling family, then your embassy walls are torn down, and you're vulnerable to attacks from the principalities and cosmic powers that want to ruin your witness. And your home is no more a refuge for the weary than a minefield. It will be filled with anxiety, anger, worry, and false peace. That's the funny thing about minefields. They look normal, even peaceful, until you step on the wrong stone. There's no real peace in a family where the believers aren't reconcilers. And whatever Holy Spirit power that could be demonstrated through your family is quenched.

But (and thank God for *buts*), if you pursue reconciliation in your home, the embassy walls will be rebuilt. Instead of your embassy being a minefield, it will become a place of shelter and real peace. And not only will your family benefit from the ministry of reconciliation, but all who enter for refuge – friends seeking counsel, or in need of encouragement, or even just the simple hospitality of inviting people in for fellowship – they will reap a benefit from the safety and security of your embassy.

And not to stretch this metaphor too far, but if you take the ministry of a reconciler seriously, as an ambassador, you'll benefit from *diplomatic immunity* on foreign soil. International law defines diplomatic immunity as the immunity from criminal prosecution and from some civil jurisdiction to diplomats and their families.[6] There's a spiritual application as well. By pursuing reconciliation, the powers of darkness will have fewer grounds for accusation, fewer footholds whereby they can ensnare you. Never treat reconciliation in your relationships as an optional thing because it compromises your diplomatic immunity as an ambassador for God's kingdom!

RECONCILIATION WILL COST YOU

If my sole concern in reconciliation is the personal cost to me, then I've started out on the wrong foot, and the process is poisoned at the roots. However, that doesn't mean it's an illegitimate question. There is a cost in reconciliation. There is no genuine reconciling that ever happened where both parties remained the same. And if one party walks away unchanged, real reconciliation did not occur. It costs *everyone* at the table something. But if the personal cost of reconciliation isn't the most critical question, then what is the most critical question to consider when you approach the task? You're probably not going to like this.

The most essential question in any reconciliation is this: *how can I serve you?* The first cost of genuine, gospel reconciliation is first, and always, your pride. If you don't come to the table in humility, recognizing your own failures, your own brokenness, your own propensity for sin, AND recognizing your own before your brother's, then just stay home and spare everyone the charade of peacemaking. You're not serious about reconciliation until you're more concerned about your own brokenness than your brother's. Consider the following.

> Blessed are the peacemakers, for they shall be called sons of God. (Matthew 5:9)

> So if you are offering your gift at the altar and there remember that your brother has something against you,

leave your gift there before the altar and go. *First be reconciled to your brother*, and then come and offer your gift. (Matthew 5:23-24)

Why do you see the speck that is in your brother's eye, but do not notice the log that is in your own eye? Or how can you say to your brother, 'Let me take the speck out of your eye,' when there is the log in your own eye? You hypocrite, *first take the log out of your own eye*, and then you will see clearly to take the speck out of your brother's eye. (Matthew 7:3-5)

Do nothing from selfish ambition or conceit, but *in humility count others more significant than yourselves.* (Philippians 2:3)

Put on then, as God's chosen ones, holy and beloved, *compassionate hearts, kindness, humility, meekness, and patience,* (Colossians 3:12)

I could keep going, but I think you get the point. Your own brokenness is far more pressing than anyone else's. Jesus emphasizes the importance of peacemaking and being reconciled to your brother, but then also says that lest you think your brother's problems are big, *yours are bigger*. Therefore, *in humility*, counting your brother as better than yourself, come to the table of reconciliation with compassion, kindness, humility, meekness, and patience. Go search it out for yourself. I've pieced together theses verses, but you'll find that this is a consistent theme through the Gospels and the letters of the Apostles that we consider our own sin as the worst, and we begin with that understanding as we approach the reconciliation table.

How can I serve you? That question doesn't ignore your hurts, it just gives preference to the wounds of the person sitting across from you. And when both people come to the table with the same heart of humility, asking the same question, *everyone's hurts will receive ministry!* But not only does that assure that everyone receives ministry, it ensures that everyone is more concerned about somebody else, rather than themselves, and Christ is exalted.

The next cost in genuine reconciliation has to do with the behaviors that led us to the table in the first place. Let me emphasize that this part is much easier when we've paid up on the first cost of our pride. In fact,

I'll go even farther: if you haven't really paid up in pride, then you won't be willing to sincerely change any behaviors. Everything in reconciliation depends on humility and loving service being the foundation. Here's what I mean.

The most striking example of reconciliation I can think of in the Old Testament is that of the prophet Hosea. God instructed Hosea to marry a woman who would be unfaithful to him. Now, I can only imagine what went through Hosea's mind when God told him that, but as a prophet, he was obedient. Now, let's be careful. That doesn't mean that Hosea went out and found the first loose woman he encountered. For the message to be heartfelt, God led Hosea to a woman who he would love. He married a woman named Gomer (Hosea 1:3).

Let's read between the lines. God is going to use Hosea to prophesy to Israel his displeasure at their unfaithfulness. God loves Israel, but she has continually cheated on him by worshiping lesser gods. His pain over this is real. Remember, God is emotional. So he calls out Hosea and charges him to love a woman who would be unfaithful to him. What I'm saying is Hosea *truly* loved Gomer. He had to, or else the message that

God wants him to convey to Israel would be unfelt and kind of hollow for the messenger.

As a worship pastor, I do occasionally get to preach. It never fails, every time I do, God gives me a message that penetrates my heart first. I feel the message before anyone else. But not just when I preach; my ministry for being responsible for the songs of my church is similar. If we sing a song at my church, it has penetrated my heart first. The messenger is nearly always first filled with the emotions that God wants his people to feel. It's no different with Hosea. Hosea married Gomer, and he loved her like God loves Israel. And that's what makes this such an excellent example of reconciliation.

Gomer does as God said she would. She leaves Hosea for another man. And God tells him to go get her back. In fact, the text implies perhaps that she had become a sex slave since Hosea had to *repurchase her*. In Hosea chapter three it says that Hosea bought Gomer back for fifteen pieces of silver, plus some wine and grain. The price for a slave was thirty silver coins [7], not fifteen, so the fact that he threw in some wine and grain means he probably spent his last dollar, plus whatever he had in his cupboards to get her back.

Think about it. She cheated on him. She left him. Hosea had every right to find a better wife who wouldn't cheat. Even with Yahweh's word that she would eventually be unfaithful, the hurt was probably still deep. Yet, Hosea loves the Lord, and though Gomer cheated, he still loves her. So, when the Lord told him to go get her, Hosea spent everything he had to get back his beloved. What does this have to do with reconciliation? It paints a picture of how we should approach the table. We should love God and love our brother enough that we are willing to lay everything down on the table in pursuit of reconciliation. If I'm willing to lay everything down to pursue my loved one, that should not only empty my pockets and cupboards, but it should temper my expectations with grace and compassion. Let me demonstrate.

When Radene and I have had our deepest, darkest battles, the only thing that kept me from picking up my sword and storming her gates is that fact that I love the Lord and I love her with every fiber of my being. That doesn't mean I didn't feel like storming her gates. Those feelings were definitely there. But I knew that an assault like that would only prove that I can hurt her more than she hurt me. Besides, the evidence of the fact that I love her so deeply is found in how she was able to wound me so deeply. Deep hurts only come from people you love deeply.

Thankfully, I have had enough godly men and women in my life who either taught me or lived out in front of me how to respond in a meek, peacemaking, reconciling way. I love Jesus enough to do what he asks, and I love her enough to not seek my pound of flesh. That produced in my heart a genuine desire to come to the table, willing to do whatever it takes to get us back to a good and pleasant place. It was the difference between:

> "You're a jerk, you hurt me, get out of my life until I feel like I can be around you again."

and

> "Honey, I love you, and I want things to be great between us, but what you did hurt me and has driven a wedge between us. *What can I do to help restore things?"*

That's what Hosea did. That's what we're supposed to do. Reconciliation costs us everything. But more importantly, it cost Jesus everything. He put everything on the reconciliation table and kept nothing for himself. His whole ministry was serving, not taking. He never demanded anything; he only came to serve. Everyone who comes to the table of reconciliation must come with nothing less than everything.

START PRACTICING

I know, you're thinking I'm naïve, I'm blowing this thing out of proportion, I'm too much of an idealist. I know you're thinking that because I used to think the same thing when others said these things to me. I would say, *"You're over-spiritualizing matters."* But when I hit a few big bumps in the journey, I realized I was sorely ill-prepared to reconcile with people biblically. I was too convinced of my own rightness, I was too bound up in pride, I was lacking humility, and it was those very things that caused me to scoff at the things I've been sharing with you. Friends, if you don't practice this in small things – when someone doesn't repay, when someone interrupts, when someone speaks carelessly, when someone isn't truthful – you'll be ill-prepared to practice this in the massive relationship problems that *everyone* is going to have. And it gets scarier. If you don't practice this in small things, in your home, in your family, in your friendships, you'll not recognize the need for larger scale reconciliation between groups of people within the church, within the community, even within the nation.

We are *reconcilers*! We've been given the ministry of reconciliation, and yet the Church is more known among the people for making (or finding) enemies than making peace. Pastor Judah Smith preached at the 2018 Gateway Conference that we are far more involved in finding enemies than we are at ministering healing to the broken. That's an indictment on how seriously we're taking the ministry of reconciliation. And it gives a glimpse into the private lives of individual believers. If we're not practicing reconciliation in private and in the community, then to maintain unity we'll unite around a common *enemy* instead of unifying around the cross.

I keep referring to the table of reconciliation. I hope if you've been a believer for long, that this has stirred up an image for you. The table of reconciliation is the Lord's Table. We remember it every time we take the bread and take the wine. We practice this sacrament to remember the reconciling work of Jesus, but we seldom come to the Lord's Table having done all we can in all of our relationships to be reconciled. We bring shame to the name and memory of Christ, and we grieve the Holy Spirit when we don't pursue reconciliation.

But let's be real. Reconciliation is a two-way street. If I were to leave you here with everything I've said, but not address this, I'd be abandoning many of us in limbo. What about those times where you desire to reconcile, but there is no desire from the other person? What about those times where you do come to the reconciliation table, but it's not an equal participation because you came in humility ready to serve, but they came with no such spirit? We have to admit and come to terms with the truth that full reconciliation isn't possible every time because no matter what, you will always have at least two broken people at the table: you and someone else. Our ruined, sinful nature will never go down without a fight, and it will *always* look for ways away from reconciliation. And sometimes brokenness wins the day. What then?

Thankfully, God knew this, and he's given us a way to make peace with a lack of peace. Jesus consistently taught that in conflict, you are the party responsible for taking the first step toward reconciliation. *If your brother sins against you, go to him* (Matthew 18:15). *If you realize you've sinned against your brother, go to him* (Matthew 5:23-24). Believers cannot escape the responsibility of making the first move toward reconciliation, regardless of whether you're the offended or the offender. So for the sake of brevity, let's assume you're making the first move in obedience to Christ's command, in humility, in an attitude of service to your brother, living out everything we've already discussed. You're sticking your neck out in love to mend fences, and all you get is a cold response or none at all. Or perhaps it goes further, but stalls at the table because they refuse to see their own brokenness. God's word has something encouraging to say to you.

> If possible, *so far as it depends on you*, live peaceably with all. (Romans 12:18)

If possible live in peace with everyone… *as far as it depends on you.* There's a clause here that accounts for the sinfulness of sin. Not every attempt at reconciliation is going to be a smashing success, so the Lord offers this little glimmer of hope. *You do what I've taught you, take the first steps, come with a spirit of humility and service, be kind, be gentle, be self-controlled, and if it still doesn't work out, you can be at peace with yourself that you did everything you could, as far as it depended on you, and my Spirit will not be grieved.* Don't be too quick to assume you've done everything you can, but also, don't destroy yourself people-pleasing your brother or sister into a quasi-peaceful relationship. God knows, and his Spirit will only be grieved if you don't try, or you give up before you've done all that you can.

A RECONCILING LIFE

Reconciliation is a way of life that's cultivated and practiced. Its seeds must be planted and cared for in loving relationship with one another. Thinking back to Moses, you could tell that his people already had a chip on their shoulder toward him.

> Who made you a prince and a judge over us? Do you mean to kill me as you killed the Egyptian? (Exodus 2:14)

For whatever reason, there was bitterness between the Hebrews and Moses. Perhaps that bitterness was all on their side. It could be that they knew who Moses was, saw his lavish life as a royal and got indignant toward him. So when he tried to appeal to them as a brother and fellow Hebrew, they scoffed at him. *Who do you think you are? You forgot where you came from! What are you gonna do? Kill me?* It sounds just like when siblings fuss with each other and say, "*Who died and made you king? You can't tell me what to do!*" See, Moses, even though he had no malice in his heart and had nothing but good intentions toward his Hebrew brothers, was far removed from their experiences as slaves. Their experiences as slaves embittered them. His experience as a royal distanced him. Neither of them were seeing things rightly. Both Moses and his Hebrew brothers needed a reconciling.

The strange thing is that God humbled Moses for the next forty years to make him ready for leading a people who once despised him. God had to work out the attitudes of privilege and entitlement that came from his royal family so that he could deal with the grumblings and complaining of the Hebrews as they wandered in the desert of Sinai for forty years. As well-intentioned as you may be, if you think you're ready to reconcile, but you lack humility, God will humble you before reconciliation happens. Reconciliation is cultivated and practiced, and I'm willing to bet that in the forty years that Moses was away from Egypt, getting married, living among a nomadic people, watching sheep for a living, he had to cultivate and practice reconciliation again and again with his wife's family. So when he actually led his people, he was a different man at eighty years old than he was at forty. And the evidence is that Moses went to the mat for Israel time and time again before the Lord. He gave the rest of his life leading a stubborn people who didn't always appreciate his leadership, through a difficult and, at times, tragic journey.

Moses did everything, *as far as it depended on him*, to love and lead the people God had given him charge over. And it cost him everything. He came to the table on one side, the people of Israel on the other, and the give and take was seldom equitable. Fast forward to your life. Who in your life have you *not even tried* to reconcile with? Who have you been at odds with, but you're afraid of the emotional toll it will take on you to come to the table of reconciliation? Or how about this one: have you been blinded to the need for reconciling with people, or even a group of people, by your own pride? If you've been blinded, fine, you were blind. But now that you're not blind, you're responsible. What's it going to be?

I know this chapter has been weighty and I've spoken very directly at times, but it is time for God's people to take up the mantle of responsibility which we've been given. We've been given the ministry of reconciliation. As firstborn sons of the Kingdom, we're reconcilers. We *proclaim* the good news that God has reconciled himself to us through Jesus Christ, but we take it to the next level and *demonstrate* the power of God in reconciling ourselves with each other! Have you ever been curious as to why the Church has fallen into such a poor reputation among the lost? It's this, it's always been this, it'll continue to be this: we're not living as reconcilers. I used to think it's because they don't like what we believe. But now I don't think that's it at all. Even if they hate what we believe, if the power of God were on display through the ministry of reconciliation in our midst, they would at the very least have to admit that what we believe actually works. Why are we called hypocrites? Most of the time it has to do with how we conduct ourselves in relationship to other people.

I'm telling you, Church, if we're ever going to be effective ambassadors and embassies of the Kingdom for the weary, we've got to sow some seeds of reconciliation in our families, in our friendships, in our churches, in our communities, cultivate those seeds, and let God bring the growth. Practice reconciling in small things so that you'll be well practiced for big things. And the bonus is, if you practice it, you'll be sharpened to recognize Satan's schemes to divide us from whatever angle he tries to slice it.

References:
1. https://founders.org/2010/03/05/memo-how-to-smoke-out-a-calvinistic-pastor-in-your-church/ accessed September 13, 2018.
2. Omniscience – having all knowledge about everything that has existed and will exist; all-knowing.
3. Omnipotence – having all power over everything in existence; all powerful.
4. Omnipresence – being present in all places in existence, and all moments in time, all at once; all-present.
5. Immutability – being unchanging or unchangeable over time in nature and character.
6. https://www.britannica.com/topic/diplomatic-immunity/ accessed October 30, 2018.
7. ESV Study Bible notes on Hosea 3:2.

LOVING THROUGH

Of all the topics we've addressed in this book, this one may be the hardest. Not because it's controversial, not because it's undesirable, but simply because it requires the most from us. This is the hard part of the journey: loving through. I heard a story once of an older woman, well advanced in years who was well known in her community for her love for Jesus, her family, and her love for her church. In fact, her reputation was so well known over the decades, that it had become a matter of local legend. She hadn't sought notoriety. She wasn't looking for attention. But the magnitude of her love was so supernatural that attention found her quite naturally. She was a local icon.

One thing that everyone knew about her is that she enjoyed spending time on her front porch. It was well decorated, and welcoming, which led to many people just stopping by for a chat in the rocking chairs that lined the wall. Age had not dulled her passion for an active social life. She welcomed guests to her porch. But not every person who walked by was interested in pleasant conversation. Her faith in Jesus was so well known, that it also drew its share of detractors and mockers (as active faith seems to do). One day, while she tended the flowers around her porch, a small group of young men were walking down her street and decided to have some *fun* with her.

They mockingly shouted to her, "You better get ready 'cause Jesus is comin'!" She ignored them. Undeterred, they shouted again, "You better get ready, I heard Jesus is comin'!" Again, she paid them no mind. This time the young men stopped and took a small step onto her lawn, trying once more to get a rise out of her. "Jesus is comin', you better be getting ready!" At this, she stopped what she was doing, put down her tools, took off her gardening gloves, and walked up to them. She motioned for the tallest one to bend down and incline his ear. As he bent, she reached up, grabbed his ear, pulled him down the rest of the way, and said in the sternest tone, "You better listen to me, I don't have to get ready. I *keeps* ready!" She let him go, he recoiled in pain, and the boys kept moving along down the road, laughing and joking, poking fun at the tall one whose ear was still red and stinging from the encounter.

I have no idea if that story is true, I only know that it was told to me and I've never forgotten it. Regardless of whether it's true, what she says to that young man is full of truth. She *keeps* ready. What does that have to do with *loving through?* And by the way, *what in the world is meant by loving through?* I'm glad you asked. First of all, *keeping ready* means that you're frequently cultivating friendship with the Holy Spirit. You're always making time for prayer – conversation – with the Holy Spirit. You're consistently concerned with the condition of your friendship with the Holy Spirit. That means you don't go long without confession. You don't go long without expressing gratitude. You don't go long without time spent just listening to him speak as you read the Word. In other words, you have a real relationship with the Spirit of God within you, and you regard him as a real person who has real feelings and real desires to know you and have fellowship with you every day. So, you cultivate that and nurture that by fostering an atmosphere of trust and realness with him. That's how you *keeps* ready. He's the most important person in your life, and the most important conversation you'll have all day, every day.

Loving through is impossible without keeping ready. This old woman's faith and love had notoriety because her readiness enabled her to love through anything. Therefore, loving through is this: regardless of circumstance, regardless of difficulty, regardless of what people will think of you, you keep loving through all things. Your love is unwavering. It's when God's perfect love for you bears fruit in your human relationships. Your love for people begins to reflect God's love for you.

> For I am sure that neither death nor life, nor angels nor rulers, nor things present nor things to come, nor powers, nor height nor depth, nor anything else in all creation, will be able to separate us from the love of God in Christ Jesus our Lord. (Romans 8:38-39)

When we begin loving people like this, we know that God's love is bearing fruit in our hearts. It's not perfect, it's not identical, but its aroma reminds the Father of his love for us. Loving one another *through* whatever may come, whatever may try to derail us, is one evidence that the love of God is present and bearing good fruit in our lives. But finding this stride, arriving at the capacity to love this way, doesn't happen without some holy blood, sweat, and tears. Hopefully, you're connecting the dots. Everything we've talked about so far – unity, sacrifice, reconciliation, and awareness of the devil's schemes – is entirely connected to and vital to our ability to love through.

WHY ARE WE BAD AT THIS?

I can't speak for believers all over the world, but I can say this about believers in America. We're terrible at loving through, and it's because we've become too comfortable in Pharaoh's house. We've considered the treasures and pleasures of Pharaoh's house too precious to part with. We've sacrificed unity for convenience. We've paid little mind to Satan's schemes in keeping us divided. Our sense of entitlement has driven us to cling to our *rights* instead of the hem of Jesus' garment. We lack the spiritual stamina to engage in Biblical reconciliation. In the large picture of God's global family, we're the spoiled siblings living in riches while the rest of the family is in poverty. And we can't even get along amongst our spoiled selves. How in the world will we endure when great tribulation arrives if we're not practiced at enduring small skirmishes with each other?

Why? Why is it so difficult for two people who love Jesus to love one another? Why is it so hard to swallow pride and offer a simple apology? Why do we feel so entitled to receiving apologies when we've been hurt? As a pastor, I've been a witness to this happening on repeat, again and again, in many different situations, among many different families and friends. And in the spirit of full disclosure, it's happened in my family as well. No one is immune. The questions we should ask when faced with these realities are, *why do I want an apology so badly*, or *why is it so hard for me to simply apologize?* I think many times you'll discover an ugly root at the foundation of both of those questions. It's too often a root of entitlement and privilege, nourished by arrogance and self-importance.

Are there times in conflict where we should plant a flag and say this far and no further? Absolutely. Sometimes for the sake of your own spiritual and emotional health, it means you have to raise a standard and say until *this* happens, we can't move forward. That doesn't mean you're no longer interested in reconciliation; it just means that the process is at a standstill until something breaks the logjam of opinions and feelings that every reconciling effort will endure. But let's call it what it is. These stalemates in our reconciliation efforts are *always* because of our sinful condition. At times people are demanding too much and laying too high of an expectation on the broken person across the table. And at others, the person on the other side of the table is too blinded by their hubris to admit they were wrong. And let me be fair to us Americans: there's family squabbling all across the family of God, worldwide. It's only that our comfort makes us especially difficult children. It reminds me of when Jesus said:

> Again I tell you, it is easier for a camel to go through the eye of a needle than for a rich person to enter the kingdom of God. (Matthew 19:24)

Oh, now we're getting somewhere. Could it be that our entitlement and wealth are what poisons the well? Is it possible that our ability to love our neighbor is intimately tied to how much we treasure our stuff, our rights, our liberties, and our little kingdoms that we build? Look at what Moses had to lose before he could love his neighbor well enough to lead them through forty years of whining and complaining. And even then, Moses struggled to love the Israelites through every difficulty. Remember this?

> And as soon as he came near the camp and saw the calf and the dancing, Moses' anger burned hot, and he threw the tablets out of his hands and broke them at the foot of the mountain. (Exodus 32:19)

> Then Moses and Aaron gathered the assembly together before the rock, and he said to them, "Hear now, you rebels: shall we bring water for you out of this rock?" And Moses lifted up his hand and struck the rock with his staff twice, and water came out abundantly, and the congregation drank, and their livestock.
> (Numbers 20:10-11)

In both of these cases, Moses lost his temper with the people of Israel for their disobedience. Now, in fairness, the Israelites were basically being jerks to God and to Moses, but he lost his temper in these moments after enduring long strides of moaning and complaining from the people. What's my point? Even after forty years of exile and humbling, where God shaped him into the kind of leader Israel would need, he managed to have his moments. And the moment where he struck the rock in anger, cost him his opportunity to enter the Promised Land (Numbers 20:12). If Moses still lost his cool after all the loss that God took him through in preparation for leading Israel, how can we, who have lost relatively little, be able to love through anything?

I'm not saying that the loss we *do* endure isn't painful. Loss is loss. And neither am I advocating that a life of poverty gives you superior spirituality. I'm not saying sell all your possessions and become destitute so that you can be spiritually rich. I'm not that guy. There are those guys out there, and I would caution you to be wary of the false teaching that wealth *always* detracts from your spiritual health. All I'm saying is that wealth, privilege, and entitlement *can* play a role in blinding us to our broken condition. Look at it this way.

Every dollar you spend on comfort is a dollar spent to cushion the blow of the Genesis three curse. Every invention ever made was crafted to lighten the sweat of our brow because of the curse. The more we invest our wealth in comfort and ease, the less aware we remain of our sinful, broken condition. And if we don't understand how broken we are, we won't understand what is necessary to love through anything that comes at us. Take away the niceties of life, and our brokenness quickly surfaces. It's the reason looting happens when the power goes off for too long in cities. It's the reason we get cranky and short with each other when the air conditioning breaks down in the heat of summer. It's the reason people swap churches so quickly when the holy trinity of Sunday School, AWANA, and Youth Group aren't functioning at full capacity… well, maybe I'm meddling now. But you know it's true! *I'm not being served to my liking, so I'll go somewhere else where I will be!*

The truth is we're never far from our brokenness, we've just manipulated and gamed the systems in our lives to keep everything moving and flowing in the direction that prevents us from feeling the curse. Interrupt that flow and see how quickly just plain ol' ugly sin erupts and destroys relationships, wrecks families, and kills peace and unity in the Body of Christ – we've all seen it, but I don't think we've always recognized it like this. So, what is the root? Why are we so shaken when the flows of our lives get disrupted? If we're going to be a people who love through every circumstance, we have to get to the root of this problem within us.

FEAR IS THE ROOT

Earlier in the book, I mentioned that Radene and I were asked by some close friends to mediate a sticky family situation they were facing. I was reluctant at first because I felt too close to the situation, but as it became clear to me that they wouldn't even try unless it was us, I agreed. We were doing our best to broker reconciliation between them, and it was an arduous, months-long process. It was tiring for everyone, and I think at some point, everyone at the table, including me and Radene, thought about cutting losses and giving up.

There is one moment in this process that I will never forget. Everyone came to the table that day, and we were trudging through feelings and opinions and hurts. It was hard, but we eventually got to a point where some apologies were finally being offered. I consider Radene a discerning person, but I'm not sure she discerned what was about to happen.

Radene asked the question to one of them, "Is your apology sincere?" What happened next was fast and furious. This person went from calm to enraged in less than a second! Radene received a sharp, angry rebuke before I could even get a single word out of my mouth. I had to raise my voice – something I don't like doing in these situations – to regain control of the table.

One calm question that was only double checking this person's integrity and honesty surfaced some severe anger and hurt.

I'm happy to report that we got beyond that moment, and reconciliation has birthed some good fruit in our friends' family. But I bring this up to demonstrate how close we are to our brokenness. That outburst didn't come from nowhere. It was there all along. The question was a pinprick that released some pent-up pressure beneath the surface. What was that pressure? Where did it come from? Why was my friend so easily goaded into anger by a question that only required a simple *yes* or *no*? I understand that no one enjoys having their integrity questioned, but the furious nature of my friend's response was out of proportion. What happened?

Fear. Fear is what happened. And without being too simplistic, I want to suggest to you that fear is at the root of *everything* in your life that keeps you from becoming the man or woman that the Father wants you to be. Fear is what hinders your growth into a Kingdom person. Fear is what prevents you from loving through any circumstance that comes in life. Love is sacrificial, and when the price tag for love is high enough, fear begins tempting us to fold and cut our losses. Let me show you how fear is the driving force of every act of disobedience in our lives.

GIDEON'S FEAR

> Then Gideon said to God, "If you will save Israel by my hand, as you have said, behold, I am laying a fleece of wool on the threshing floor. If there is dew on the fleece alone, and it is dry on all the ground, then I shall know that you will save Israel by my hand, as you have said." And it was so. When he rose early next morning and squeezed the fleece, he wrung enough dew from the fleece to fill a bowl with water. (Judges 6:36-38)

I've been in church long enough that I've heard this story explained in Sunday School and preached in sermons many times. And almost every time this is preached or taught, it is centered around God's faithfulness to Gideon and to Israel. And that is true. If you've heard a sermon, or if you've taught a lesson that way, you were on solid ground. But seldom have I ever heard anyone speak of Gideon's disobedience. And if you know the story, this first sign wasn't enough for Gideon, but he tested the Lord once more asking for the fleece to be dry and the ground all around to be wet (Judges 6:39-40). And the Lord did as Gideon asked, which is a testimony to his faithfulness. But this scene is *not* an example of Gideon's faithfulness.

What never seems to get talked about is Gideon's disbelief, which adds a layer of depth. God told Gideon in verse fourteen that he would use him to defeat Midian:

> And the Lord turned to him and said, "Go in this might of yours and save Israel from the hand of Midian; do not I send you?" (Judges 6:14)

Now, I've heard many of my friends in the Church say, *if God said it, that's good enough for me.* And everyone around says, *Amen.* But that apparently wasn't enough for Gideon. And the truth is, it's not good enough for any of us. Out of fear and disbelief – disobedience – Gideon asked God for a sign. We do the very same thing. Oh, we don't shear a sheep and lay out the fleece on our patio furniture; we do more spiritual things. We ask God to give us *peace* about what we're going through. We ask God to make us feel a certain way as a sign that we're on the right path. We've turned a sense of peace into our fleece, and until we get that, we let fear paralyze us in the journey, putting us at odds with the Spirit of God who is telling us to move.

Let me tell you something. The Garden of Gethsemane wasn't peaceful. Jesus wasn't asking for a sense of peace and calm. He was beating his fear into submission with courage and determination. He knew the will of the Father, and he wasn't asking God for a *feeling of peace* about the situation. He was turning to the Father for *strength* and *courage* to endure the hostility he was facing. Sure, he asked for an alternative solution, but he was quick to say, *"Not my will but yours."* Instead of asking God for an emotional sense of peace, we really should be asking for courage to stand firm and endure the onslaught. The peace you seek doesn't always come up front. The famous line of the psalmist, *"Be still and know that I am God,"* (Psalm 46:10) is a psalm of war. And in the middle of it, God says *be still*. Here, peace comes in the middle of the battle, not before it begins.

The need for God to give you a sign is rooted in fear. If his Word is truly good enough for you, then stop asking God to prove himself. He already has. It is our task to believe his Word and act upon what he has already said.

Gideon was filled with fear, but let's be fair, he was facing an enormous task that would make any of us fearful. That's why God was merciful toward his disbelief and gave him the signs he asked for. But let's look at something a little less intimidating; something a little less threatening than an army of Midianites. What about your reputation?

ANANIAS AND SAPPHIRA'S FEAR

> But a man named Ananias, with his wife Sapphira, sold a piece of property, and with his wife's knowledge he kept back for himself some of the proceeds and brought only a part of it and laid it at the apostles' feet. But Peter said, "Ananias, why has Satan filled your heart to lie to the Holy Spirit and to keep back for yourself part of the proceeds of the land? While it remained unsold, did it not remain your own? And after it was sold, was it not at your disposal? Why is it that you have contrived this deed in your heart? You have not lied to man but to God." When Ananias heard these words, he fell down and breathed his last. And great fear came upon all who heard of it. The young men rose and wrapped him up

and carried him out and buried him.

After an interval of about three hours his wife came in, not knowing what had happened. And Peter said to her, "Tell me whether you sold the land for so much." And she said, "Yes, for so much." But Peter said to her, "How is it that you have agreed together to test the Spirit of the Lord? Behold, the feet of those who have buried your husband are at the door, and they will carry you out." Immediately she fell down at his feet and breathed her last. (Acts 5:1-10)

Ananias and Sapphira are a special case. This was early in the church, maybe only several weeks after Pentecost. People who were being saved were selling their possessions and donating all the proceeds back into the church to help the needy. This was happening so much that apparently Ananias and Sapphira decided they wanted on the bandwagon, but they didn't want to give *all* the proceeds to the church, just a portion of it.

Let's be clear. There was nothing wrong with what they wanted to do. No Apostle had commanded the believers to sell their properties. These were spontaneous offerings of goodwill that people were giving freely. So, there was no command, no expectation, no *anything* that was compelling Ananias and Sapphira to sell anything at all. It was on their heart to do so. But where this goes south is their decision to deceive the church. They brought the money and lied about keeping some for themselves.

Why lie? Even Peter asked that question: *"While it remained unsold, did it not remain your own? And after it was sold, was it not at your disposal?"* The answer is, of course, fear. They were afraid that their reputation would suffer among the people in the church. They feared they would appear selfish. They feared they would look greedy. So they tried to preserve their reputation, motivated by that fear, by attempting a lie. Apparently, God chose to take this moment to teach the young church a lesson. This lie cost them their lives, and God called them home right there on the spot in front of everyone. Fear is beneath even the little white lies that we tell to boost our reputations. Let's look at one more.

GEHAZI'S FEAR

> But when Naaman had gone from him a short distance, Gehazi, the servant of Elisha the man of God, said, "See,

my master has spared this Naaman the Syrian, in not accepting from his hand what he brought. As the Lord lives, I will run after him and get something from him." So Gehazi followed Naaman. And when Naaman saw someone running after him, he got down from the chariot to meet him and said, "Is all well?" And he said, "All is well. My master has sent me to say, 'There have just now come to me from the hill country of Ephraim two young men of the sons of the prophets. Please give them a talent of silver and two changes of clothing.'" And Naaman said, "Be pleased to accept two talents." And he urged him and tied up two talents of silver in two bags, with two changes of clothing, and laid them on two of his servants. And they carried them before Gehazi. And when he came to the hill, he took them from their hand and put them in the house, and he sent the men away, and they departed. (2 Kings 5:19b-24)

Elisha had just healed Naaman of leprosy. Naaman had brought an extravagant amount of silver and gold to bless the prophet for healing him, but Elisha refused to accept any gift and sent him on his way.

Gehazi got all out of sorts about this. Gehazi saw the money and expected that Elisha would receive at least some of it. But when he didn't, all of Gehazi's hopes for what they could do with that wealth got flushed down the drain. Out of fear – *fear of not getting what he wanted from that wealth* – he chased down Naaman, lied, and took some of the silver for his own personal gain. Then he returned to Elisha and got called out for his sin.

> He went in and stood before his master, and Elisha said to him, "Where have you been, Gehazi?" And he said, "Your servant went nowhere." But he said to him, "Did not my heart go when the man turned from his chariot to meet you? Was it a time to accept money and garments, olive orchards and vineyards, sheep and oxen, male servants and female servants? Therefore the leprosy of Naaman shall cling to you and to your descendants forever." So he went out from his presence a leper, like snow. (2 Kings 5:25-27)

Fear of loss – in this case fear of losing something you don't even have – motivated Gehazi to lie, steal, lie again, and his sin caught up to him. What's going on in each of these scenarios? Fear convinces us that God isn't going to be enough. Fear convinced Gideon to doubt God and ask him for signs. Fear persuaded Ananias and Sapphira that their reputation with the church folks was more important than honesty before the Lord. Fear of unfulfilled desire motivated Gehazi to lie and steal because simply being right before the Lord wasn't fulfilling enough. There are so many more we could examine to prove that sin is rooted in fear, but if you recall, we covered this earlier in chapter three. *If Satan can tempt you by convincing you that you're missing out on something... aren't you falling prey to the same temptation he used on Eve? Isn't that a fear-based pursuit? Eve was afraid she was missing out on something that God was holding back from her, so she took Satan's bait.*

The root of humanity's sin is found in fear. And when we face trials, we are tempted by fear to check out, to withhold, or to attack. It's a fear of more hurt, of more loss. It's a fear that if we don't get the advantage and attack now, we'll lose control. Since we love control, fear works on us, because if we can control what happens to us, then we think we'll have *peace.* Fear cripples us from loving through because loving through always includes letting go of control, and if you think controlling your life is what will bring you peace, then you'll *never* love through difficulty.

That was a mouthful, and a hard truth to wrestle with. I know people, and so do you, who apart from a Jesus miracle, will go to their graves trying to control the people in their lives so that they can have the kind of peace that *they* want: a life where nothing challenges them, nothing rocks their boat, nothing takes them by surprise… that sounds an awful lot like a god-complex. There's only one person who is never challenged, never rocked, never taken by surprise, and his name is Jesus Christ, Son of the Living God. Therefore, if you are controlling, you're playing god, and it never fails: you are a terrible god. To love through, you have to release the reigns of control. You have to come to terms with the truth that *you* are the only person you can control, and even in that, you must cede that control to the Holy Spirit. If you can't let go of control, you prove that you are full of fear and unable to love through like Jesus.

GOD'S LOVE REMOVES FEAR

> So we have come to know and to believe the love that God has for us. God is love, and whoever abides in love abides in God, and God abides in him. By this is love

> perfected with us, so that we may have confidence for the day of judgment, because as he is so also are we in this world. *There is no fear in love, but perfect love casts out fear. For fear has to do with punishment, and whoever fears has not been perfected in love.* (1 John 4:16-18)

We'll walk through this, but look at the last verse first, and then we'll back up. *There is no fear in love, but perfect love casts out fear. For fear has to do with punishment, and whoever fears has not been perfected in love.* Got fear? If you are living in fear, then you've not allowed the love of God to work in your heart. But what does that mean? Let's jump back to verse sixteen.

> So we have come *to know and to believe* the love that God has for us.

To *know* and to *believe* are not the same things. The word *know* that is used here is actually used in a very broad sense to mean several things.[1] It's used to speak of understanding and perception, as in you understand and perceive how something works, or how to explain something. It's used in other places to mean getting to know someone, as in a relational knowledge of another person. Then in other spots, it's a Jewish idiom for sexual relations: Joseph did not *know* Mary until after Jesus was born (Matthew 1:25). So here's what we can say about knowing the love of God.

Knowing the love of God means that you have intimate knowledge. You're understanding and perceiving it as you journey with him. You are growing in it as you get to know him. You're spending time in the Word, with the Holy Spirit and allowing him to shed light into the dark places within you. It's the knowledge that is learned from time spent, and miles journeyed with the Lord.

The word *believe* is actually simple: to have faith.[2] So, what you *know* about God's love will move you to greater *belief* in his love. If you *know* little, you'll *believe* little, but if you *know* much, you'll *believe* much. Here's how that plays out practically.

There was a time in my life where I cared too much about the opinions people had of me. Those cares had deep roots in the rejections that I experienced as a child from some of my peers. As an adult, I guess you could say I was eager to please people for the affirmation my childhood self was denied. I was blinded by it, and when Radene would try to point it out, I always had a justification for whatever my choices were. But as I walked with the Lord and grew in my understanding of his love for me, the opinions of others became less important.

Increasingly, defying my need for affirmation became an action of faith – a faith that was informed by what I knew about God's love for me. When I was tempted to be a people pleaser, it was a step of faith for me to refuse, and trust in the affirmation that God provides, and not men. That's just one issue of too many to tell you about, but it was a big one! Look at the next part of verse sixteen.

> God is love, and whoever abides in love abides in God, and God abides in him.

God is love is abused by the world, turning God into someone who never judges us, never asks us to change, and never denies us the things we want. But in reality, that abuse of the Scripture is just a reflection of the kind of selfish love that we have for ourselves. We don't want people to judge us, we don't want to change for people, and we always want what we want, so we impose that kind of love on the sort of god that we hope Yahweh is. But let's bring it back to the text.

God is love isn't an exclusive statement. It doesn't mean that he's *only* love, it just means that all of what love is can be found in him. And then the rest is easy. If you have come to *know and to believe* in God's love for you, then you live in God, and God lives in you! Let me make it plainer. God's love is so great that anyone who knows and believes in him like we've talked about, will be filled with that same love, and it will be evident that God lives within you. Let's keep moving.

> By this is love perfected with us, so that we may have confidence for the day of judgment, because as he is so also are we in this world.

When you see *by this*, the first question you should ask is this: *by what?* By *what* is love perfected with us? By *knowing and believing the love God has for us.* By *abiding in God's love.* So then, how does knowing, believing, and abiding in God's love for us perfect us? And what is John saying when he says we are perfected? We are taken through a process of change – the Bible calls it sanctification.

> But now that you have been set free from sin and have become slaves of God, the fruit you get *leads to sanctification* and its end, eternal life. (Romans 6:22)

The love of God *will not* leave us the same way it finds us. If you came to God a drunk, his love won't let you remain a drunk. If you came to God a thief, his love won't allow you to stay a thief. And it's because knowing, believing, and abiding in his love *will* transform us into new people. And this transformation becomes a source of confidence for our day of judgment. It will be evidence that Jesus was at home in our hearts, living through us, and increasingly so the longer we journeyed. In fact, that is the meaning of the statement, *as he is so also are we in this world*. The more we are sanctified by his love, the more we become *just like him in this world*.

Loving through is made increasingly possible as God's love casts out fear from our lives. The roadblocks to loving through any situation are always centered around the fear that you'll lose, or that you'll not get what you think you deserve if you don't *do something about it*. Sometimes we feel like we are the ones who have to teach someone a lesson, but really that is disguised hurt and anger. We can make it sound spiritual because we've become experts at masking our real feelings with Bible verses. But in the end, we're just afraid. We're afraid that if we don't get what we want that we'll lose control.

Loving through lets go of control. It doesn't budge on truth, but neither does it use truth as a mechanism to maintain control. How do I know that? Because Jesus *still* loves me, despite my failures, my seasons of rebellion, my premeditated sin, despite everything I have done, am currently doing, and will do. His love is unwavering. He doesn't change. Also, he doesn't change the truth to accommodate my feelings about matters. But he doesn't arm twist me into submission either. He gently, calmly calls me to repentance, even while he allows my troubles to dogpile on top of me as I try to control my life the way I want. He patiently waits for me to journey back. God's love never fails, never ceases, never shifts, never stops for a breather, it is unrelenting and undeterred by my failures. And with that in mind, we should remember this:

> A new commandment I give to you, that you love one another: *just as I have loved you*, you also are to love one another. (John 13:34)

Do you love this way? Jesus said this to his disciples, even to Judas who would betray him later that evening. Do you think Jesus loved Judas through to the end? Yes.

> ...having loved his own who were in the world, *he loved them to the end.* (John 13:1b)

Again, I ask, do you love this way? The honest answer is, at best, *sometimes*, because this isn't natural. This kind of love is supernatural, and that is why we must keep ready. The old woman from the story I told at the beginning of this chapter, if real, grew in this kind of love just like we must. Her fears were methodically cast out as God's love perfected her. And the more fearless she became, the more she was able to love through anything. She fought for unity, she discerned the devil, she laid down her privilege and entitlement, she faithfully pursued reconciliation, and by working all of those spiritual muscles through her years, she grew in her capacity to love through any situation, just like Jesus. In fact, it was Jesus loving through her because she had learned how to die so that he might live.

Loving through isn't just an exercise of spiritual strength, it's the desire of the heart of every believer with pure devotion to Jesus, even if you aren't yet skilled at living it out. But as you progress on your journey, and you let the Holy Spirit use your difficulties and trials as anvils for shaping your new self, there will be a change. You'll love through with increasing steadfastness. But perhaps most importantly, the power of God will be evident in the love you demonstrate throughout whatever may come. You could say it is the official language of the Kingdom of God. It's no wonder that Jesus told his disciples,

> By this all people will know that you are my disciples, *if you have love for one another.* (John 13:35)

References:
1. Strong's number: g1097
2. Strong's number: g4100

YAHWEH'S HOUSE

I've spent considerable time and space in this book telling you how Pharaoh's house can ruin us. It compromises our empathy, it threatens our unity, it tempts us with privilege and entitlement, it blinds us to our responsibility to reconcile, and it destroys our capacity to love through any circumstance. I've tried to keep drawing us back to Moses and what he had to lose before he could be the man that God needed. And I think I've done that in a way that's understandable and applicable. But if I ended it here, you might walk away discouraged, and I don't want to leave you hanging on an unresolved thought. There is more to say about our condition that will lift our gaze away from our brokenness up toward the prize.

The Christian life isn't just about loss. Is there loss? There must be. God allows us to endure loss, division, and strife, for one glorious end: that we would become like Jesus. One of Paul's more confusing statements from 1 Corinthians says that there *must* be divisions among you so that those who are mature can become evident (1 Corinthians 11:19). Indeed, loss and struggle are promised to the person who is born again into God's kingdom. But what we endure isn't just for suffering's sake. Every hardship you and I suffer as men and women of God's kingdom is repurposed to destroy the remaining vestiges of our sin, thus preparing us for living in a new home, a new house: Yahweh's house.

Yahweh's house stands in contrast to Pharaoh's house. Pharaoh's house was built on the backs of slaves, but indeed, everyone who dwelled in that house became slaves to its power, luxury, and privilege. Even Moses was affected, but quite dramatically, God took him away from that setting to transform him into a servant, usable for his glory. Yahweh's house is a house of service where people aren't advanced by merit or ambition, but instead *the last will be first, and the first will be last* (Matthew 20:16). It's a house where *the greatest among you is a servant* (Matthew 23:11). On the day we enter that house for permanent residency, people will be denied entrance and will protest that in Jesus' name they *performed many signs and cast out many demons* (Matthew 7:21-23). In Pharaoh's house, those merits might have gained you a seat at his table, but in Yahweh's house, they get you nothing.

Jesus spoke about his Father's house to the disciples on the night before his crucifixion. He said:

> In my Father's house are many rooms. If it were not so, would I have told you that I go to prepare a place for you? And if I go and prepare a place for you, I will come again and will take you to myself, that where I am you may be also. (John 14:2-3)

The King James Version of the Bible says, "In my Father's house are many *mansions*." Most English translations render the verse with either rooms, dwelling places, or mansions. Take your pick because the Greek simply means *residence*.[1] So Jesus has been preparing a residence for everyone who is born again into God's kingdom. Is it any wonder that the vision John had in Revelation of the New Jerusalem had such epic dimensions (Revelation 21:15-17)? Whether we should interpret those dimensions literally isn't the point. The point is that the home we will have with the Father in his kingdom will be vast, and there will be room for everyone who placed their faith in Jesus in this present age.

In contrast, Pharaoh's house was for a select few. His table had no seat for the slave. Pharaoh's house was small. His house will always produce *haves* and *have nots* and will favor the *haves*. As long as we choose his table over Yahweh's, neither will we have room for the oppressed at our tables, and we too will remain small and only favor people who are like us.

A HOUSE THAT REDEEMS

Let's do this. Let's talk about Yahweh's house. (And forgive me if I swing too much between the phrases *God's kingdom* and *Yahweh's house*. I'm going to use them interchangeably because for our purposes here they mean the same thing.) In many ways, we've trained ourselves to think about heaven in a negative way. Not negative as in it's a bad experience, but instead we tend to think about what *won't* be there. There'll be no more sickness, no more injustice, no more death, no more poverty, no more evil; a bunch of *no mores*. And rightly so. The Bible speaks of all of these *no mores* and offers them to us as a contrast to our earthly experience.

But for many of us, our thoughts of Yahweh's house stop with what will be absent. The kingdom of God is much more than an opposite experience to our earthly life. In fact, *opposite* isn't even a good adjective to use. Though there will be experiences in Yahweh's house that are opposite of our experiences in Pharaoh's house, it's actually more helpful to think of those things in terms of being *redeemed* instead of being opposite. For example, consider adoption.

Moses was adopted into Pharaoh's house. Let's be fair as we speak of this: it was a blessing. For everything that it may have done to corrupt and distort Moses' worldview, it was still a great blessing. God used it to give Moses an education, an understanding of leadership, but more than those things, it was an act of preservation. Pharaoh had decreed that all male Hebrew newborns were to be cast into the Nile (Exodus 1:22). So God orchestrated Moses' adoption into the royal family of Egypt to protect him, to educate him, to prepare him for delivering Israel from Pharaoh's rule. But it also turned him into an Egyptian royal, with all the privileges and entitlements that come with the family.

That's what adoption does. As someone who was adopted, I can relate to this. But over the years I've met more and more people who were adopted, and I've come to realize that my experience was mild in comparison. I was adopted within my family. People who are adopted into entirely different families testify of drastic changes, considerable differences in their environment. But regardless of the degree of difference, the same thing happens. When you're adopted into a family, you typically become like the people who adopted you. You're still you, but you become a new you. Adoption transforms you into a person who picks up some of the characteristics of your new family.

Unfortunately, while sin still dominates our world, for all of its merits adoption isn't perfect. As much as it can and does rescue, often the broken nature of the parents and the child work against the good things that it can build. In other words, both our good and bad qualities are shared. They both come to bear in the transformation of an adopted child. And the child brings all of their hurts and wounds to the adopting family. Everyone is changed, and the challenge is to overcome the brokenness of both parent and child. In truth, that's the challenge for all parents and all children, whether adopted or naturally born.

But, in Yahweh's house adoption isn't held captive by sin. When we are born again, we are adopted into a family where the Father has no sin to pass to us. It's a family where our own sinfulness doesn't change the Father. In fact, our elder Brother has taken responsibility for all of our sins and received all of the condemnation that we would otherwise – in any other family – had to bear ourselves. Yahweh's house transforms us into people like our Father, which means that the more we get to know him, the more time we spend with him, the less we will be like the person we were prior to our adoption. There is absolutely no negative, no down-side, no gotchas, nothing that we receive in this adoption that would contribute to our brokenness. But instead, everything we receive plays a role in healing and getting us back to an Edenic relationship with our Creator where he can *walk with us in the cool of the day* as he once did with Adam and Eve.

And isn't that the point? When you zoom out, and you consider all of the activity of God in human history, what is the point of it all? God created this entire universe, and in its vastness and endless beauty, he formed a planet, put some water on it, put some land on it, and planted a garden on it where he could spend time with his two prized creations – Adam and Eve. He walked in the garden with them, in the cool part of the day and fellowshipped with them. That's the opening chapters in Genesis 1 and 2. Look to the closing chapters of Revelation, 21 and 22. What do you see? You see God on the earth, living among his people as he did in the beginning.

Can I paint a huge stroke here? Everything that Yahweh does between those bookends has one guiding purpose: adopt a family who will live with him in his house for eternity. The saga of redemption begins with him dwelling with his human family, and it concludes the same way. Since that is the case, our experience of redemption can only do one thing: *make us ready for Yahweh's house*.

Do you see how God redeems the concept of adoption? Human adoption is a great thing, but it's imperfect because of sin. When God adopts, the downside doesn't exist. He takes something that's broken in our world and transforms it for his kingdom. So that opens up a great question. What will redeemed humanity be like? How will it function? What will daily life in Yahweh's house look like? For sure, there are things we can't know so I won't be able to answer every question that can be asked. No one can. But the Word of God still tells us *many* things.

WHAT DOES REDEEMED HUMANITY LOOK LIKE?

We began this journey discussing Pharaoh's house. While this isn't the case for every believer on the planet, as American Christians we have lived as Moses did in Pharaoh's house. Blessed for sure but led astray. Corrupted by the freedoms, material possessions, and luxuries that Pharaoh's house affords us. America is Pharaoh's house (and oh my, this could preach for a long time). Example: Pharaoh was killing the babies of the most oppressed people under his rule. America enables baby killings for anyone who wants one, which statistically hits minorities (the oppressed) the hardest.[2] But that's not where I want to go... just had to slip that one in to demonstrate the analogy.

The corruption I speak of has been demonstrated throughout this book. Pharaoh's house at best distorts and at worst destroys unity, breeds privilege and entitlement, ruins the potential for reconciliation, wrecks our ability to love through differences, and makes us blind to the role of Satan in our downfall. And remember, the world does this by nature... I'm only talking about Yahweh's people. These things are inside the walls, beyond the gates, and are wreaking havoc on the inside of the Body of Christ. And the sad thing is that many of us are convinced that we are righteous in our mindset. We use the Scripture to our advantage and prop up our pathetic, pseudo-biblical arguments that release us from the obligation to be the one who actually stands up against injustice and defend the oppressed. Many have looked to pragmatism and political action for answers instead of Jesus Christ who would lead us toward the brokenness and evil in people, and not away.

So, before I get lost in this, let me reel myself in and get to the good stuff. The good news is God *is* redeeming our brokenness. Yahweh's house will be a house of justice. It will be a house of righteousness. Reconciliation will be fully realized in all of our relationships. We will have perfect unity. And though we will indeed have privilege, it will never lead to entitlement because in God's kingdom the greatest among us will be a servant. It will be a culture of deference to one another and to Jesus Christ. It will be something that we've experienced only in type and foreshadow in our current lives, but then it in its most perfect expression. Let's begin our dive into what Yahweh's house is like in a familiar passage.

Love is patient and kind; love does not envy or boast; it is not arrogant or rude. It does not insist on its own way; it is not irritable or resentful; it does not rejoice at wrongdoing, but rejoices with the truth. Love bears all things, believes all things, hopes all things, endures all things.

Love never ends. As for prophecies, they will pass away; as for tongues, they will cease; as for knowledge, it will pass away. For we know in part and we prophesy in part, but when the perfect comes, the partial will pass away. When I was a child, I spoke like a child, I thought like a child, I reasoned like a child. When I became a man, I gave up childish ways. For now we see in a mirror dimly, but then face to face. Now I know in part; then I shall know fully, even as I have been fully known.

So now faith, hope, and love abide, these three; but the greatest of these is love.
(1 Corinthians 13:4-13)

We're so accustomed to hearing this passage at weddings that we become shortsighted about its relevance. This has application far beyond how a husband and wife should love each other. Think of this in terms of *all* relationships, and you'll start to get the perspective that Paul had in mind. This is the kind of love that we should have in every relationship: *patient, kind, unenvious, unarrogant, selfless, non-irritable, non-resentful, truthful, load-bearing, faithful, full of hope, and enduring.* Why should this kind of love be so paramount? Because that's how Yahweh has loved us. And if he has loved us in this way, then we should love each other likewise. This will be the tone of all relationships in God's kingdom. It's the kind of love he's trying to build in us during this life because this is the kind of love that will lead others toward the Gospel where they can find salvation for themselves and adoption into Yahweh's house.

Notice that it says *love never ends*. Love is the enduring characteristic of all God's family into the eternal age. Things that are important for the function of God's church in this age, like prophecy, tongues, and knowledge, won't be necessary for the future kingdom. Those things are important now because they are gifts that lead us, who are physical, toward spiritual realities that we can't understand left to ourselves. When God's kingdom is fully established, the physical and the spiritual realm will become one (I'll get to that in a moment), undivided, forever mixed, forever bound together as one realm. And love will endure into that age and continue to define every relationship in the Kingdom.

Paul describes our experience in this age as child's play. Our speech, our thoughts, and our understanding are clouded, marred by sin, corrupted by the flesh, and tempted by the forces of darkness. Even the smartest and most mature among us, compared to what we will know and experience in God's kingdom are still children in their ability to reason and think as spiritual people. But in the fully realized Kingdom of God, when we forever move into Yahweh's house, we will no longer know *in part* but will *know fully*.

That's all fine and dandy for the future, but what does that mean for us now? Remember a few chapters ago when I referred to our homes as embassies of God's kingdom and how the Scripture actually describes us as ambassadors? As ambassadors, we represent Yahweh to humanity. If he loves this way, then we too should love like this. If our citizenship in his kingdom means that we will become people who love this way, then that makes it *very* relevant to our experience in the here and now.

How's your love? How well are you representing Yahweh to the world by how you love people? Oh, and let me go this far: even in your disagreements, when you are at odds with another, when you are under opposition, how's your love? That's the real barometer of your love: how does it fare when it isn't reciprocated? How well does it go under attack? What kind of stamina does it possess when your beliefs about morality are constantly offended?

MARRIAGE IS THE KEY TO GOD'S LOVE

Friends, I'm not saying for one second that I have this all together. I have many days when I fail in my love for others. But I can tell you this. God has persuaded me that what I have embraced as *good enough* in the past falls far short of what he is trying to form within me for today. In Yahweh's house, love is the overarching characteristic. There is justice, there is righteousness, there is holiness, but love is elevated to an exalted place in the pantheon of God's virtues. It doesn't lessen any of his other qualities. It makes him no less strict a judge, no less vengeful against sin, and no less holy in his character. In fact, to our fleshy, worldly reasoning, God's love affects his other characteristics in counterintuitive ways.

God's love makes him a just judge. God's love fans the flame of his vengeance against sin. God's love makes his holiness accessible to unholy sinners. How does that make sense?

Let me introduce you to a concept that only makes sense in the lens of marriage. Jesus calls himself the Bridegroom (Matthew 9:15). In Revelation, the Lord refers to his people on several occasions as the Bride (Revelation 18:23, 19:7, 21:2, 21:9, 22:17). This is why the church is often called the Bride of Christ. Revelation 19:9 speaks of the Marriage Supper of the Lamb. This will be the day where all of God's saints (holy ones) from history will be united finally with their Savior, Jesus Christ in a glorious union where he is the Bridegroom, and we are the Bride.

The concept is this. The covenant of human marriage was given by Yahweh to be a foreshadowing of the union between Christ and his people. In human marriage, the husband loves his bride above all other women. Or at least that's the way God designed it. Take my marriage as the case and point. I have several women in my life who I consider friends, who I love and who I would go to great lengths to help if they were in need. But there is only one woman who gets covenant love from me, Radene, my bride. So, when push comes to shove, the other women in my life who I love and count as friends will always lose if I must choose between them and Radene.

It's the same with Jesus and his Bride. People have somewhat misused John 3:16 to forge a very poor understanding of how God loves the world. God indeed does love the world. He sent Jesus to die for humanity's sins so that all of creation could be redeemed. He isn't willing that any should perish, but that all should come to salvation (2 Peter 3:9). But his love for the world, in general, isn't the same as his love for his Bride in particular. Stay with me, here's where it may get a little bumpy.

How can I say this? If Jesus loved everyone the same, he would either be unfaithful to his Bride by loving everyone with covenant love, or he'd be unfaithful to his Bride by loving her with less than the covenant love that he promised her. The marriage relationship between Jesus and his Bride naturally means that he loves his covenant people with a different love than those outside the covenant. Therefore, because marriage reflects Jesus and the Church (Ephesians 5:31-

32), just like I love Radene before all others, Jesus loves his Bride before all others.

Now, let's connect this to the rest of God's characteristics. Look at the end. What do we see? We see the Beast and the False Prophet cast into the Lake of Fire (Revelation 19:20). We see Satan cast into the Lake of Fire (Revelation 20:10). We see Death and Hell cast into the Lake of Fire (Revelation 20:14). Then we see anyone whose names were not found in the Book of Life cast into the Lake of Fire (Revelation 20:15). It is the systematic removal of sin and the forces of darkness from the spiritual and physical realms. Every principality, every demon, every antichrist, Satan himself, even Death and Hell are removed from the realms and put in the Lake of Fire. Then lastly, people who remained in their sin upon their deaths whose names were not found in the Book of Life, are cast into the Lake of Fire.

Why the vengeance? Why such harsh justice? Look what comes next.

> Then I saw a new heaven and a new earth, for the first heaven and the first earth had passed away, and the sea was no more. And I saw the holy city, new Jerusalem, coming down out of heaven from God, *prepared as a*

bride adorned for her husband. And I heard a loud voice from the throne saying, "Behold, the dwelling place of God is with man. He will dwell with them, and they will be his people, and God himself will be with them as their God. He will wipe away every tear from their eyes, and death shall be no more, neither shall there be mourning, nor crying, nor pain anymore, for the former things have passed away." And he who was seated on the throne said, "Behold, I am making all things new."
(Revelation 21:1-5)

But nothing unclean will ever enter it, nor anyone who does what is detestable or false, but only those who are written in the Lamb's book of life. (Revelation 21:27)

Here's where I've been heading with this point about God's love. All those people who died in their sins, all those demons and Satan, all Death, all Hell, and any power of darkness that I'm missing, are cast into the Lake of Fire to prevent sin from ever inflicting damage upon God's family and his creation again! Why? Because Yahweh loves us with an undying covenant love! *The greater the love, the greater the hatred against things that would do harm to the objects of your love!* How can God send all these people into a Lake of Fire... people who John 3:16 says he loves? Because he loves his Bride with a greater love than he loves the rest of the world. And that's why I say that God's love is exalted because it is his love for his Bride that moves him to judge sin with such finality. His love doesn't supersede or exclude any of his other characteristics, but instead it intensifies them and gives them a sharper edge.

YAHWEH'S HOUSE IN YOUR HOUSE

Yahweh's house is a house of love, and we should be a people of that love which has been lavished over us in Jesus Christ. How does that change the way we live now? God's love provokes him to action, and so should ours! Look again at this verse.

> A new commandment I give to you, that you love one another: *just as I have loved you*, you also are to love one another. (John 13:34)

Ushering in the Kingdom of God in our world means becoming people who love as God has loved us. Believe me, I am not underselling the difficulty of this.

We are all works in progress. Our capacity to love this way only grows as we walk closely with the Lord. Yahweh's house will be filled with people provoked to action by love, but not the broken, selfish love-of-being-loved version that plagues us in this life. We will be filled with, made whole by, and moved to action through the redeeming love of Christ within us.

Let's pause. I've expended a lot of words talking about love and building a case for God's greater love for his covenant people, and how his covenant love permeates his house and the people who dwell there. Let's ask ourselves some questions before moving along.

Take a look at your life over the last few weeks. Take note of your relationships; your marriage, your children, your friendships, your neighbors, your coworkers, and even your enemies. In each of those categories, how well would you say that you've demonstrated John 13:34? *Love one another: just as I have loved you.* Ask the Holy Spirit for help. He'll show you the truth. As you do that, let's consider what exactly *just as I have loved you* means.

Let's deal with the most obvious first. He loves us enough that he laid down his life for us. He took the wrath of God against sin in our place. It should be us receiving that wrath, but Jesus stepped in, received our wrath, and died our death. Now, of course, we can't do that for other people. I can't die for Radene's sins, and she can't die for mine. That's what Jesus did on the cross. But Christ's ultimate sacrifice should lead me to love sacrificially in multitudes of smaller ways. And the Word is full of admonishments to do just that. In practical terms, put others first. How have you put the interests of others ahead of yours in the last couple of weeks?

> Do nothing from selfish ambition or conceit, but in humility *count others more significant than yourselves.* Let each of you look not only to his own interests, but also to the interests of others. (Philippians 2:3-4)

Jesus has loved us sacrificially. Jesus has also accepted us unconditionally. I want to be careful because this one can get derailed if it's taken the wrong way. Unconditional acceptance can be misunderstood to mean that we are accepted as is, with no obligation to change. That's not what the Word teaches. As we've already discussed, adoption into a family brings with it changes. We are changed because we're adopted. We *will* be transformed into people who look, speak, and act like our adopting Father. That's the litmus test for true faith. Is there growing evidence in your journey that you're becoming more like the Father?

Therefore, when we say Jesus accepts us unconditionally, here's what it means. First, it means you don't have to get your life right before he'll accept you. That's huge! So many religions teach that if you do x, y, and z God will receive you into his good graces. Usually, x, y, and z tend to be laws and morality that you have to practice before you're accepted. That's not what Jesus does. Read through the Gospels and take note of the kinds of people that Jesus reached. Crooks, prostitutes, sexually immoral, diseased, uneducated, unrefined, and the like are the people that Jesus reached! Never did he look at one of them and demand they clean their act up before he would heal or minister to them. He reached them as they were. He does the same for us. There's no code, there's no checklist of to-do's, there's no up-front cost of admission. The only thing you must do to receive salvation is confess and believe.

> Because, if you *confess* with your mouth that Jesus is Lord and *believe* in your heart that God raised him from the dead, you will be saved. For with the heart one believes

and is justified, and with the mouth one confesses and is saved. (Romans 10:9-10)

Second, the unconditional acceptance found in Jesus is future-proofed. That means his acceptance of you encompasses the whole of your journey in this life. Practically, that means as you walk, when you stumble it doesn't decrease, negate, diminish, or detract one iota from your acceptance with God. How can *that* be? That's because the Father's acceptance of you into his family isn't based on your moral performance, but on Jesus' life, death, and resurrection. So our stumbles in the journey are fully covered by Christ's work.

NOW... be careful to not use that beautiful truth as a reason to believe that our morality doesn't matter. Remember: those who are adopted are *guaranteed, promised, assured, and inevitably* going to become like the Father who has adopted them. It isn't overnight, it is a progressive transformation that happens over time, but it absolutely does happen, and it begins from the moment you confess and believe.

So, how has your acceptance of others fared over the past few weeks? Have people had to live up to your standard or have you been gracious and full of mercy with the people in your life?

Let's look at one more thing about how Jesus has loved us. He has loved us sacrificially, he has accepted us unconditionally, and he has also gifted us generously. What does that mean? It actually covers a lot of territory, but I'm going to zoom in on two things. First of all, in this life, Jesus has given us *everything we need* to live in ways that please the Father and advance his kingdom through the Holy Spirit. As we encounter difficulties, if we stumble through them it isn't because we're lacking in spiritual gifts and resources to thrive under pressure. Through the Holy Spirit he's given us spiritual gifts (Ephesians 4:8), he's given us every spiritual blessing (Ephesians 1:3), and he's invested his authority in us to be on mission (Matthew 28:18-20). So, we literally have no recourse to say that we weren't equipped with what we needed to do the good works that God prepared for us to do (Ephesians 2:10). The responsibility we bear is to avail ourselves to everything he's deposited within us.

The other way he's been generous is mind-blowing. He is the only begotten Son of God, meaning he's firstborn and he will inherit *all things*. Everything seen and unseen is Christ's inheritance… all of creation, both spiritual and physical. Every realm belongs to Jesus as his inheritance. And the mind-blowing thing is that he will share that inheritance with us as a *co-heir*.

> The Spirit himself bears witness with our spirit that we are children of God, and if children, then heirs—heirs of God and *fellow heirs with Christ*, provided we suffer with him in order that we may also be glorified with him. (Romans 8:16-17)

We will be co-heirs of everything that Christ inherits. Mind. Blown. I can't comprehend that reality without breaking my brain. Somehow, I will be a co-inheritor of everything that Christ will inherit. All realms, seen and unseen, will be a part of my inheritance. I don't know what to say to you except that if you don't know Jesus, you're going to really miss out.

How then does Christ's infinite generosity change our generosity? In the last few weeks, have you been generous the way that Christ has been generous with you? Don't narrow that down to just money – although generosity isn't less than what you do with money – it encompasses everything. Have you been generous with time? Have you been generous with compassion? Have you been generous with money? Christ's generosity enables us to be the most generous people on earth. If you haven't been, what is stopping you?

THE FATHER WILL LIVE WITH US

Yahweh's house is a house unlike anything we've experienced in this life. And God is preparing us to live there as we journey. Everything we've talked about so far – covenantal and sacrificial love, unconditional acceptance, unlimited generosity – these things will characterize life in God's kingdom. But talk about life in God's kingdom wouldn't be complete without pointing out the best thing about it.

Yahweh will be there.

> And I heard a loud voice from the throne saying, "Behold, the dwelling place of God is with man. He will dwell with them, and they will be his people, and God himself will be with them as their God." (Revelation 21:3)

I love beating this drum because it gets back to the essential truth of what this whole saga is about. God has been working, ever since he created the first cherub that would dwell with him around his throne, to fix a dilemma. How can he live among his creations and his wrath against sin not destroy them? In Eden Yahweh dwelled with us until we sinned, then he mercifully distanced himself, but promised redemption would come through the seed of the woman (Genesis 3:15). The journey was long, but God patiently worked out his plan, through broken, sinful and seriously flawed men and women, and when the fullness of time came, the final, ultimate Redeemer, Jesus Christ was born. His life, his death, and his resurrection solved the dilemma. When history finally arrives at Revelation 21:3, Yahweh will descend to the earth – an earth that has also been redeemed and recreated – and make his personal residence with the men and women who believed and were adopted and redeemed in Christ.

That's the endgame, folks. When Yahweh moves in next door we will finally have every tear wiped away, pain will be a thing of the past, death will be undone and destroyed, and everything that made life and this world broken will be removed. And that is just the beginning of what life in God's kingdom will be like! Revelation chapters twenty-one and twenty-two paint a lavish visual of what it will look like, but the everyday life experience of it has already been revealed to us in the teachings of Jesus and the Apostles. How will we live? Simple: read the Sermon on the Mount, read the

Kingdom Parables, read how the Apostles instruct us in kingdom living. Observe how Jesus has loved us. That is how we will live every day in Yahweh's house.

We face a profound choice. Are we willing to abandon Pharaoh's house for life in Yahweh's house? The pleasures and benefits of Pharaoh's house sabotage our ability to live as ambassadors of God's kingdom. If you belong to Jesus, but you're clinging a little too tightly to the privileges and benefits of your earthly citizenship, you'll always find yourself at odds with and frustrated by God's Word. Not all of it, but there will be things in the Word that confuse and make you uncomfortable because you've not entirely moved out of your room in Pharaoh's house. Like a college student who keeps a few things in his bedroom at home, just in case he needs to crash for a weekend, you still have a few things in your room in Pharaoh's house, just in case you want to visit for a while. You're not ready to let go completely. And that ultimately will cause you troubles that you would otherwise not experience. You have divided affections.

The challenge that every believer faces is to go all-in for Yahweh's house. We're supposed to represent that house; be a light of that kingdom. But we cripple our ability to do that by remaining too tied to this world. I'm not advocating a disregard for worldly things. Neither does Jesus. What I am promoting is a prioritizing of our citizenships. So does Jesus.

> But seek *first* the kingdom of God and his righteousness, and all these things will be added to you. (Matthew 6:33)

Let me wrap this up with a few questions that I want to leave you with. Have you allowed your kingdom citizenship to inform your earthly citizenship? Have you allowed politics and social pressures to mold you more than the Word of God? Do you read the Word of God through an ideological/political lens, or do you let the Word of God read you and change you accordingly? Have you misused the Word to shield you from dealing with difficult people, or do you allow the Word to lead you toward ministering to difficult people? Do you show mercy, compassion, and forgive people who you think will do the same for you, or do you do it for anyone regardless? How well are you representing Yahweh's house as you seek reconciliation and work to love through every difficulty?

God isn't expecting perfection from you. Jesus did that for us. But he does expect that as you walk with him, you move your things out of your room in Pharaoh's house and make your home in his house.

There are no failure to launch cases in God's family. Moses created circumstances for himself that made his move very abrupt (and very literal). And Yahweh met him, picked him up, and over time made him into the man he wanted. That's what he does for us. He patiently guides us and makes us ready for life in his house. He never fails to move us from faith to faith and glory to glory because he has promised to complete his work in us.

> And I am sure of this, that he who began a good work in you *will bring it to completion* at the day of Jesus Christ. (Philippians 1:6)

That promise provides strength enough for you to leave Pharaoh forever and throw your everything into that dwelling place that Jesus has prepared for you in Yahweh's house. It can be scary, but if you trust that Jesus has made a spacious place for you, it will unquestionably never cease to satisfy and thrill your soul to follow him.

References:
1. Strong's number: g3438
2. https://www.guttmacher.org/infographic/2017/abortion-rates-race-and-ethnicity

CONCLUSION

I always try to write the conclusions of my books *very last*. Makes sense, right? Here at the end I want to be a little vulnerable with you. In the process of writing this book, toward the end, some family drama cropped up between Radene and I and some extended family members. It's one of those things I mentioned where something I wrote was put to the test. In fact, to be very specific, it all started maybe a few weeks after I completed the chapter on reconciliation. How appropriate!

I wish I could tell you that things have been resolved. They haven't. And as I sit here composing this, there aren't any clear signs that there will be a resolution any time soon. It's not for lack of trying. Right now, there are some foundational differences in how we see things that prevent us from moving beyond this point in our reconciliation. It's a situation where I haven't lost hope, but I've come to realize that nothing is going to move forward until the Lord moves things.

Why do I bring this up? Because I think it's essential that you know I'm a real guy with real problems. I don't just get on high horses about things in which I have no experiences. It grieves my heart that reconciliation has been elusive in this situation. But yet I have peace. I have confidence that Jesus will win, and that it will be worth the long wait. How can I have that confidence? That's simple. He's done it before, and he'll do it again. Jesus has been faithful, and I've learned that my timescales are usually too short for him to work out what he needs to work out in me and everyone else involved.

What about you? As you've read through this book, what has the Lord shown you? Whatever it is, let me encourage you: if Jesus highlights something in your life that needs change, he has already provided everything you need to make that change. He doesn't show us our broken things and then leave us to our own devices to fix it. He always supplies the means to rebuild. If he shows me a crack in my wall, he also shows me where the trowel and mortar are for repairing.

He doesn't do it for me. I pick up the trowel, I apply the mortar, but as I do, he guides me.

Many are afraid to pick up the trowel. They're aware of what Christ has provided, but they're too scared of making a bigger mess. I understand that fear. But let me remind you.

> There is no fear in love, but perfect love casts out fear. For fear has to do with punishment, and whoever fears has not been perfected in love. (1 John 4:18)

I ended chapter one asking if you're ready to swim upstream, against the world, against the powers of darkness, and even against comfortable Christians. Practicing everything we've discussed in this book will require that you let go of fear. But you'll never let go of fear until you've bathed yourself in the love of our Father. Yahweh has loved us with an everlasting love through Jesus. If you doubt his perfect love for you, fear will always have a home in your heart.

It's also entirely possible that you've come to a stark realization. You're so filled with fear that you can't see how the love of God has ever been real to you. Jesus has been a guy who does amazing and great things for a lot of people, but it's never really worked out for you. I don't want to overdramatize this, but maybe you feel on the outside because you actually *are* on the outside. Perhaps you've been in the church your whole life, and it feels familiar and homey, but on the inside, you're afraid that someone is going to figure out that you've been faking it. You've never felt what others feel. You've never had the assurance that others talk about. And your fears have never really been stilled like others claim about theirs. Maybe you really don't know him.

Today you can. Confess to the Father with your mouth that you're a sinner and you need the salvation that Jesus Christ provides. Believe in your heart that the Father raised Jesus from the dead and that he is alive today! The good news of the Gospel is that it really is this simple. And if you confess with your mouth and believe in your heart, you will be saved (Romans 10:9). Once you're saved, Jesus sends the Holy Spirit to dwell within you, and ONLY THEN will there be power in your life to overcome the fears that dominate you.

If you're going to swim upstream against the world, against the powers of darkness, and *especially* against comfortable Christians, you're going to need some fearless faith from the Holy Spirit. He will supply it. You just need to pick it up and start making a mess because the journey upstream will splash people who don't want to be splashed and inconvenience people who don't want to be bothered. Trust in the Lord as you journey, be wise, be innocent, and most of all love the people who are with you, and who are against you. Recognize the schemes of Satan. Work for unity. Kill privilege and entitlement within yourself. Be a reconciler. Love through all things. And set your eyes on the City and Kingdom that is coming.

www.ingramcontent.com/pod-product-compliance
Lightning Source LLC
LaVergne TN
LVHW051728080426
835511LV00018B/2938